□□□□□

www.itchymanchester.co.uk

Globe Quay Globe Road Leeds LS11 5QG
t: 0113 246 0440 f: 0113 246 0550 e: all@itchymedia.co.uk

City Editor	Kate Statham
Editors	Si Gray, Ruby Quince, Mike Waugh, Andrew Wood
Design	Matt Wood, Chris McNamara
Contributors	Siobhan Bennetts, Leah Byrne, Matt Collins, Julia Houston, Kay Johnson, Marc O'Donnell, Nick Ritchie, Daniel Stubbs, Robert Tebb, Sarah Valentine
Acknowledgements	Azy, Dominic Betmead, Sereen El Jamal, John Drape, Darren Laws, Luke, Reuben Webb, Tim Ellis

contents

top fives

✳ **KEY103** feel the noise

Oh my God we're good to you...

Not only do we write funky little books but we also offer you, the discerning entertainment junkie, some pretty fine stuff on-line.

Point your browser to **www.itchycity.co.uk** and we'll not only keep you entertained with stories and reviews about what's going on in your city, we can also send you regular emails and SMS messages about the stuff you're into. So, we'll keep you informed about where the best happy hours are, when Oakenfold's next in town or where you can find a kebab at 2am. There's also a chance for you to contribute your views and reviews and get free stuff in return (we are too good to you). Have a shoofty. Go on.

Go to www.itchymanchester.co.uk, click on itchyme, and sign up for:

Cheap Drinks / offers • Cheap Eats / offers • House & Garage • Techno & Electronica • Jazz, Soul, Reggae & Funk • Indie • Metal & Alternative | Hip Hop, R'n'B & Breaks • Drum n' Bass & Jungle • Sixties, Northern Soul & Motown • Seventies, Eighties & Disco • Pop & Rock • | Classical & Opera • World, Folk and Latin • Gay • Comedy • Stage • Art • And all the venues we feature in the book

itchy box set

Oh, imagine. **All 16 titles**, an encyclopaedia of entertainment across the country, all wrapped up in a glorious multi-coloured special box. Every title below in one mother of a box. Limited edition, naturally, and so exclusive, we don't even know what it looks like ourselves.

Artist's impression. Is this what the box will look like?

If you were to buy these individually, it'd cost you a bargainous £44. But hello, what's this? We're doing the full caboodle **for a mere £35**, including free postage and packing. **Call 0113 246 0440** and order by credit/debit card and we'll whizz one over to you.

bath birmingham brighton bristol cambridge cardiff edinburgh glasgow leeds liverpool london manchester nottingham oxford sheffield york

itchy cities...

Glasgow

Edinburgh

Leeds

York

Manchester

Liverpool

Sheffield

Nottingham

Birmingham

Cambridge

Cardiff

Oxford

Bristol

London

Brighton

Bath

www.itchymanchester.co.uk

manchester 2002

Indisputably Britain's 2nd city (Birmingham, it's about time you gave it up), Manchester clearly has bags to offer everyone from the passing executive to the full-time loafer, but where to begin? Last year, itchy Manchester 2001 gave you the lowdown on what was hot, what was not, what was a hit, and what was well…shit. But so much has changed. There's the Commonwealth Games 2002 of course, the

fully functional Printworks (cinema complex with lots of soulless bars), The Great Northern, an abundance of café bars, loft apartments and a whole host of new club nights. And that's before we've even mentioned the council's sudden veer towards fuddy duddyism in abandoning support of all the music festivals (sort it out will you?). Well, we've rewritten the whole goddamn thing from start to finish to make sure that if it's on, it's most certainly in.

Slender Manchester's centre (unlike that of its dirtier and uglier cousin, London) can be circumnavigated in just over an hour. But that would obviously be a waste of valuable drinking time, so we've divided it up for your ease and pleasure into sections for bars, pubs and shopping…

Northern Quarter – cool Manchester. Think NME, think A&R, think art, urban casual, cute plaits, rare vinyl, cult fiction, Belgium beers, pretension, clichés….

Deansgate – townie, officey, hair down, knees-up and maybe a quick scrap for good measure.

Castlefield & Deansgate Locks – bliss for summer drinking, as long as you don't breath in (oh, the sweet smell of Manchester's waterways).

Triangle/Printworks – all new, all posh and all totally without character.

Arndale – yuk.

King Street & Business District – well scrubbed, well heeled, all the smartest fashion-wear and all the poshest restaurants.

For those who dare to escape the jowls of the city centre (or aren't lucky enough to live in a swanky loft apartment yet), we've also checked out the best of the leafy suburbs of South Manchester…

Fallowfield – a graveyard in the summer – Fallowfield is students, students are inescapably (oh if only) Fallowfield.

Withington – oh dear. Bless. Not much here – but plenty of buses out.

Chorlton – Go straight to IKEA, do not pass Moss Side, aim to earn over £200 per day (my body is a temple…).

Didsbury – very posh houses for media luvvies and advertising executive couples – no shops but lots of uninspiring chain-café bars.

West Didsbury – boasts quality urban-chic clothing, numerous excellent restaurants and four blindingly good beer gardens. Me biased? Never.

In a hurry? We've studiously reviewed every bar, restaurant, pub, club, bowling alley etc in town, but here's a run-down of the highlights of this fair city.

■ ■ Two hours

Manchester deserves more. Where you going that's so important eh? If you really can't stick around for longer, your best bet is to take a wander around the Northern Quarter – a Manchester institution. Trot along Oldham Street hunting down rare and collectable vinyl (recommended are Vinyl Exchange and Fat City) and have a fruit milkshake in Café Pop, or something proper to drink in Dry.

■ ■ A blow out weekend

OK, so you're having it large over the weekend. Here's the run-down of what's what.

Stay: At the Portland Thistle, or maybe Malmaison. Not cheap, but they're both centrally located and a cut above your usual bed and breakfast fare. Go on, treat yourself.

Shop: In two days you can barely scratch the surface of Manchester retail outlets. You could spend a whole day record shopping for a start. For clothes and pretty things that cost a fortune head for The Triangle, followed by King Street, and the soon to be opened Harvey Nicks.

Attractions: To get out of the city centre, take the tram to The Lowry, or if you want to stay central, head for The Museum of Science and Industry. The Fletcher Moss Park is very scenic and boasts a cute little café too, slightly further out and you'll get to Alderly Edge – cute little village and lots of footballers walking their dog action as you're in proper Cheshire territory now.

Eat: There's loads of really good restaurants in Manchester – to suit any taste or budget. Highly recommended are Dimitri's (Greek), Palmiro (Italian), The Lime Tree (British), Fat Cat for snacky lunchtime grub, or Greens for vegetarians.

Drink: Deansgate Locks is lively at the weekend (although a bit townie), Castlefield generally is great for summer nights, and Centro or Bar Cord in the Northern Quarter are the perfect places to sample that too-cool Manchester vibe.

Club: Electric Chair (Music Box) or Friends & Family (Roadhouse) are a must if you're in Manchester when they're happening (see itchymanchester.co.uk for listings), or if pulling is a priority then Loaf, Tiger Tiger or Piccadilly 21's won't fail to deliver (unless you want decent music too).

■■ A seriously cheap weekend

It's not the cheapest of Northern cities, but you can experience Manchester without needing to extend your overdraft (too much). If you give yourself £125 to spend in a weekend, here's what we recommend you spend it on…

Stay: Stay somewhere like The Merchants Hotel which is just off Oldham Street – very central, very basic, but very kind on the wallet. £50 (for a single room for two nights at the weekend)

Shop: As little as possible, obviously. But you could always pick up some obscure fashion item at Afflecks Palace – pretty cheap (what d'ya mean coz no one else would wear it?). £5 (if you're not fussy)

Attractions: Manchester Museum is free, and you might even learn something. Failing that, The Roman Fort, Central Library and The Town Hall will all let you browse around without charging you for the privilege. £5 (some money for buses to save those little legs)

Eat: Dr Livvys at Dry Bar's not at all bad, and very reasonably priced. Others worth a try over the weekend are The Craft Centre, Café Pop, Tampopo (really nice but not very expensive), and let's not forget Abduls kebab houses are everywhere. £25

Drink: If you've got NUS you're sorted – there's more student pubs than you could possibly crawl round – and all very cheap. For those of us who pay taxes, try happy hours at Soft or Down Under, or Baa Bar is the cheapest Deansgate Locks option (£1 a shot). £35 (generous or what?)

Club: Manchester has actually been turned into one big café bar, and fortunately, most

of these are free entry all night. Clubwise Planet K is very cheap, and Matt & Phreds, Dry and Night & Day are all practically free – you've got a wide choice of venues, so just avoid the big clubs like Sankeys. £5 (will get you in anywhere!) **Total: £125. Sorted.**

✳ **KEY103 feel the noise**

restaurants

www.itchymanchester.co.uk

Manchester knows how to cook – that's official. Despite our penchant for ripping into places that do a shockingly bad job, we could only find a few criminal venues this year, which is no bad thing. Meal for two prices are the cost of 2 x main course plus a bottle of the cheapo house wine.

■ ■ American

■ ■ Hard Rock Café
The Printworks (0161) 831 6700

Hard Rock Café is predominantly a theme bar/restaurant but it's also Manchester's own museum of rrrrrock. It's all pretty gaudy looking – neon lights, big TV screens, fairy lights, gold mirrors, all the usual American tack. The staff are all far too bubbly and giddy – 'have a nice day' and all that, as they constantly loiter around your table. The food is bog standard American theme stuff – burgers, burgers, and more burgers. Oh, and some chips. A characterless, cholesterol-stuffed homage to all things American, and over-priced with it.
Daily 12-11.30, Fri-Sat bar till 2am
Meal for two: £23.65 (Pig Sandwich)

■ ■ Nandos
The Printworks (0161) 385 8181

Imagine if McDonalds were to shorten their menu to just a Chicken Sandwich, but offered it in different degrees of spice, or with different types of potatoes, or possibly for the more adventurous, a chicken burger with rice – well, then you'd be close to the Nandos style of restauranteering. You order your food from the counter, get your own cutlery, wash your hands in the restaurant and have to get up every time you want another drink. Which means there's very little I can tell you about the service, as it's non-existent, just like the atmosphere – apart from the blood curdling cries of other peoples' little darlings. Nan-dos is a Nan-don't I'm afraid.

Sun-Thu 12-11.30, Fri–Sat 12-12
Meal for two: £22.85 (Half Chicken with two sides)

■ ■ British

■ ■ Grinch
5/7 Chapel Walks (0161) 907 3210

Sick of eat-by-numbers chain restaurants? Sky-painted ceilings, wrought iron chandeliers and strawberry hand soap are a few little touches that set this restaurant apart from the rest. Situated in a competitive business-lunch location, Grinch continues to be one of the most popular restaurants for lounging shoppers, office workers, romantics and afternoon eccentrics. Reasonably priced, with great coffee and tasty fodder, prepared perfectly and served with a smile. Oh, and Jim Carrey thankfully has nothing to do with it, phew.

Mon-Sun 12-11pm
Meal for two: £25.85 (Fried Chicken)

■ ■ The Lime Tree
Lapwind Lane, West Didsbury
(0161) 445 1217

Even the fussiest of eaters can't find fault with this wonderful restaurant in the leafy suburb of West Didsbury. The waiters will recommend a drink to compliment each course, and they can even be trusted to choose a fine bottle of wine for you based on limited knowledge of what you're after. Alcohol aside, the menu is only limited to make the choice between one delicious dish and another slightly easier for you. By some

miracle, having eaten three equally fantastic courses, you will be left feeling perfectly satisfied. A sophisticated and intimate atmosphere – but you will absolutely have to book first. If you want to impress someone (or scarier still, that special someone's parents), then take them to The Lime Tree – you'll become very popular indeed, trust us.

Tue-Fri, Sun 12-2.30, Mon-Sat 5.30-10, Sun 6-10pm
Meal for two: £32.85 (Cajun Fillet of Salmon) – early evening menu available before 7pm

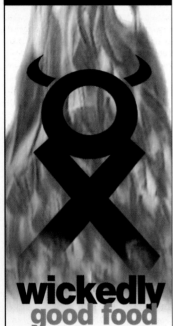

■ ■ ■ The Lincoln
Lincoln Square (0161) 834 9000

The Lincoln, as one of Manchester's more up-market eateries, caters for special occasions, as opposed to those 'can't be arsed to cook' ad-hoc meals. You can tell too – you won't find those floor-to-ceiling glass frontages in McDonalds you know. Inside it's a modern, clean affair, with top-notch food, an innovative menu and professional and efficient service. Lunches are more affordable with set menu prices.
Mon-Fri 12-3, Mon-Thu 6-10.30, Fri-Sat 6-11, Sun 12-4
Meal for two: £40 (Monkfish)

■ ■ ■ The Living Room
Deansgate (0161) 832 0083

Always a queue to get in here at the weekend but what are your options? Bar Med? RSVP? Don't think so. This is the best of a bad Deansgate lot, and once you get in, it's not so bad after all. It's very Casablanca in style, little palm tree things, banquet seating, and a baby grand. They serve up a fine array of cocktails, and have a fine array of cocktail waiters. The restaurant area is fenced in and cosy, and if you're lucky you could find yourself dining next to the likes of David Beckham or Andy Cole (did I just say lucky?).
Mon-Thu 10-1am, Fri-Sat 10-2am, Sun 10-12
Meal for two: £31.40 (Salmon Steak)

■ ■ ■ The Ox
**71 Liverpool Road, Castlefield
(0161) 839 7740**

Now this you must try. OK, The Ox isn't the most inviting name for a restaurant, but it's more a traditional pub so the name's quite

■ ■ Sarasota
Canal Street (0161) 236 3766

Situated above Mantos, away from the crush of Canal Street, Sarasota is the perfect place to go on a balmy summers evening… get a window seat and enjoy the engineering feat of retractable ceilings. Actually it's a top-notch idea, allowing you to feel the fresh evening air without being windswept. Until the rain, snow and sleet come pissing down onto your chips anyway. Plenty of variety, prices on the high side, but overall a high standard of food in attractive surroundings.
Mon-Sat 12-3, 5.30-12am, Sun 5.30-11pm
Meal for two: £39.85 (Fillet of Lamb)

fitting. Think rich reds, deep purples, old wooden tables, cosy alcoves, inviting fire – all the attractions of tradition without the traditional stench of old dog and pipe smoke. When it comes to the food, it's equally appealing and value for money. Three-course Sunday roasts set you back a tenner, but you're paying for the love and attention that's gone into each roasted morsel. Relax, take your slippers and indulge yourself.
Mon-Sat 11-11pm, Sun 12-10.30
Meal for two: £32.15 (Rack of Lamb)

■ ■ Market
104 High Street (0161) 834 3743

Over 20 years old and still going strong, Market is a landmark of taste and upmarket food with staying power. The menu's modern British, but they've kept it comfortable and cosy, which can only be a relief after the chrome and glass overload of many other city centre joints. Charming, delicious and just a tad pricey. The a la carte menu changes bi-monthly.
Wed-Fri 6-9.30 (last orders), Sat 7-9.30
Meal for two: £37.85 (South East Asian Salmon Fishcakes, wine – litre)

■ ■ Simple
Tib Street (0161) 835 2526

Opened in June 2001, Simple is owned and run by the same people that brought us Box Bar (which unfortunately at the time of going to press has been Boxed-off – see itchymanchester.co.uk to see if it's going to come out of hibernation). Simple, décor-wise, is just that. Tables and chairs scattered around a small but airy space on Tib Street, just off Oldham Street. The original idea was that it would primarily be a restaurant/bar, but as trade during the day veered more towards coffee and light snacks, they've expanded their repertoire to include those too. A very calm and quiet ambience, with views out onto the Northern Q types rushing by. Simple provides a clean and sophisticated addition to the area's bars and restaurants.

Mon-Thu 11-11, Fri-Sat 11am-12am, Sun 11am-7pm
Meal for two: £19.50 (Sausage & Mash)

hello again, the food's a bit of a let-down too – mediocre dishes and flavours no less. The only real emotion felt during an evening here is the bitter sense of being cheated when the bill arrives. A word of advice; prepare to be served by the most attentive staff in Manchester. They either love their job or they thought I was trying to steal the cutlery.
Daily 12-2.30, Mon-Fri 5.30-10, Sat 5.30-11, 6-9 Sun
Meal for two: £41.50 (Roast Goosnargh Chicken)

■ ■ ■ Simply Heathcotes
Jacksons Row, Deansgate (0161) 835 3536
Hello, what's this? White-washed walls, odd blocks of primary colours, and weird plastic heat-moulded garden chairs. Aha, it's art, I see. Décor in here does nothing for us whatsoever, but it appeals to the thespian types that frequent the place. To give you an indication of the prices – frankly out of order. But, before you write this place off, you should know that Michelin-starred chef Paul Heathcote is behind the cooking, which means a range of traditional dishes with a contemporary twist (naturally, ahem). But

■ ■ ■ French

■ ■ ■ Beaujolais
70 Portland Street (0161) 236 7260
A rather unassuming little Frenchie. Squeezed amongst some Chinese restaurants on Portland Street, Beaujolais looks like a pretty grotty bistro from the outside, but the food inside has been raved about by food critics and the general public alike. It's not as cheap as its appearance suggests but if it's quality, authentic French cuisine you're after

then this is the place to eat. Booking is advisable, especially at weekends when the joint is teaming with hungry punters. Midweek is perfect for couples, as the cosy interior and aphrodisiac-laden ingredients are sure to add a touch of ooh la la to your evening.

Tue-Fri 12-2, Mon-Fri 6-10.30, Sat 7-11
Meal for two: £42.40 (Steak au Poivre)

■ ■ ■ Café Rouge
82-84 Deansgate (0161) 839 0414

Ah now, I like this. For a start, you don't have to queue to get in, and unlike the other bars on the Deansgate parade, this is purely about eating, chatting and having a nice meal in a nice environment. No big drinkers, no loud music, no snogging in the corner. Yeah, it's trying to be a French café when it's not really French, and no one who works there is French, and the food isn't really French, but who cares? The lighting is low, the setting is right. In an ideal world, you'd be able to sit outside, settle yourself in a wicker chair, sup a cold beer and watch the world go by. But it looks out onto Deansgate, so live with it.

Mon-Sat 10am-11pm, Sun 10am-10.30pm
Meal for two: £27.60 (Poulet Dijon)

simple
an urban bar/restaurant

quote 'itchy' when booking your table and receive a complimentary bottle of wine

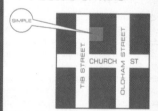

0161 835 2526

Unit 20-21
Smithfield Building
Tib Street
Manchester N4

■ ■ ■ Chez Gerard
43a Brown Street (0161) 214 1120

Brown leather and tan sofas, huge artsy vases, glass, subtle individual table lights, low coffee tables and immaculate dining tables – no wonder the suits love it. At lunchtime, the whole place buzzes with the business trade it predictably attracts, and at night the restaurant is busy with couples, pre-theatre goers and larger groups. It's worth seeking out for non-diners at night though, as they've got a huge selection of cocktails, and during the afternoon it's a really relaxed and scarcely populated place to grab a cup of coffee and a snack. However, if you are dining – the food here is very accessible French cuisine. The wine list features New World wines as well as the classic French labels.
Mon-Sat 11-11. Closed Sunday.
Meal for two: £29.85 (Toulouse Sausage)
HH: various offers and happy hours,
changes weekly.

■ ■ ■ Le Petit Blanc
Off King Street (0161) 832 1000
Petit Blanc brasserie opened last November and we can confirm that for once, their PR machine hasn't been too far off the mark. Following in the footsteps of the Oxford and Birmingham branches, Petit has launched into the heart of the business district and caters well for suits and sprogs alike. Modern and stylish interior with huge vases of flowers, clean modern lines and a spacious layout that still allows privacy. Eugh, this is sounding like a press release…but there really isn't much to fault about the place. Food was extraordinarily tasty and reasonably priced, and the service genial. Recommended.
Mon-Sun 11-11
Meal for two: £42.15 (Lemon Soul)

■ ■ ■ Reform
Spring Gardens (0161) 839 9966
Make up your mind why don't you? One minute you've closed down, next minute you're open again, then you're changing owners and so on and so forth. Well, you've

had the cast of Hollyoaks and Corrie up in arms, their social life has been in a right state. Still, you're open now and that's all that matters. Nothing inside seems to have changed. Same old velvet drapes, sensuous sofa seating, huge gold chandeliers, cheeky leopard print decoration. It looks gorgeous, the food is gorgeous, the staff are gorgeous, and last time I looked you had to pay to go to the toilet. All very London like with prices to match. Mummy, when I grow up, I want to eat at Reform.

Mon-Wed 12-11, Thu-Fri 12-2am, Sat 6-2am
Meal for two: £51 (Atlantic Swordfish)

■ ■ ■ Chinese

■ ■ ■ Oriental Buffet
48 Whitworth Street (0161) 228 1313
Situated in the basement of one of those

huge Whitworth Street buildings, inside, they've clearly gone for modern, simple, stylish décor. Shame then that they've ended up with a grim, motorway service station interior. Still, if you can close your eyes and forget your surroundings, the food's reasonable and plentiful, with an all you can eat £6.50 lunch and £8.50 evenings. Most definitely not sumptuous, but not a bad idea for big groups and value for money for fat bloaters.

Daily 11.45-10.30pm
Meal for two: £25.80 (all you can eat buffet)

■ ■ ■ Pacific
58 George Street (0161) 228 6668

It's not implausible that you'll spot the odd A-list celebrity in this contemporary and forward thinking restaurant, as it's building a reputation as one of the best pan-Asian eateries in the city. Pacific's originality is reflected in the idea of Thai food on one floor and Chinese on the other – the décor varies between the floors from modern clean lines to a more traditional setting, but is stylish on both. Eating here is a tad more expensive than the nearby competition – but it's a price worth paying.

Mon-Sun 12-3, 6-11 for Thai, 12-11.30 for Chinese
Meal for two: £44.50 (set banquet)

■ ■ ■ Yang Sing
Princess Street (0161) 236 2200

Following two years at a temporary home due to the IRA bomb, it has now returned to its spiritual home on Princess Street and has been described by cultural commentators as being 'probably the best known Chinese restaurant in the country.' This is, of course, an outright lie. Still, it's an extensive two-floor facility: bright and light with dutiful, efficient service. The owners Gerry and Harry Yeung work hard to produce some of the finest Chinese food in Manchester. A wide selection of starters range from about £3-£7, the soups are superb and the main courses are simply divine costing about £7-£13. Always busy and bustling with satisfied customers, this restaurant caters particularly for daytime business with delicious Dim Sum served until 4.30pm, and also offers a good selection for vegetarians.

Sun-Thu 12-10.30, Fri-Sat 12-12
Meal for two: £47.60 (Cantonese Fillet Steak)

■ ■ ■ Indian

■ ■ ■ Cachumba
Burton Road, West Didsbury (0161) 445 2479

An unusual, comfortable and relaxed little eatery. The menu is a mixture of African, Indian and Thai and it's all delicious – including the desserts. Almost something for everyone – the swordfish steak is sublime if you're a fish fan, the various daal, ochra and bean dishes are all fantastic if you're veggie, and the red coconut curry is one of the best I've ever had. The prices are very reasonable, and it's bring your own too – so the perfect place to bring a date if you're a bit strapped for cash. The restaurant is based on a Moroccan feel and is a really pleasant place to eat, but it is small – so book ahead for the weekends.

Mon-Sat 6-9.30
Meal for two: £9 (Red Coconut Chicken Curry). BYO

■■■ Ghurka Grill
198 Burton Road, West Didsbury
(0161) 445 3461

If you're sick of your run-of-the-mill Rusholme curry experience and want a menu with a bit more originality, look no further. They know their stuff in here – the choice and quality of the dishes is beyond fault, and if you don't recognise half of the menu (as you probably won't) the very gracious staff will give you a hand without making you feel daft. Well worth getting in a stack of dishes between you to properly sample the delicious and unusual menu. Of course, as with most of the restaurants in this area, it all gets too busy too quickly, especially at weekends, so get booking.

Mon-Thu 6-12, Fri-Sat 6-1am
Meal for two: £19.90 (Sandeko – meat salad with finely topped chillies)

■■■ The Great Kathmandu
Burton Road, West Didsbury
(0161) 434 6413

This was one of the first restaurants on Burton Road, and like Great Kathmandu, it's still standing as proud as ever. Old school décor with a 'cram 'em in' policy adds to the usually cracking atmosphere. Thankfully, the chefs know their stuff too, and dish up a fine and tasty selection of Indian and Nepalese treats. As with most decent restaurants, it gets busy, fast. Especially on Sunday lunchtimes.

Mon-Sun 12-2.30, 6-12
Meal for two: £21.95 (Mis Mas Makhanwala)

■■■ Rusholme
(it's an area, not a restaurant)

Ahhhh, the infamous curry mile. Manchester does curry pretty damn well, and if nothing else Rusholme pays homage to our commitment to consuming more Chicken Tikka Masalas than you can shake a naan at, in this, Manchester's very own Indian interpretation of Blackpool seafront. It's not all flocked wallpaper and surly waiters either, although it's still definitely there in some places if you long for the grotty and moody curry experience. The selection of curry houses down this strip ranges from the absurdly cheap to downright obscenely expensive, from the licensed to BYO, and in and amongst the numerous venues, from the startlingly polite to the breathtakingly rude. Although there's a few award winners (even though it was four years ago and the management's changed twice since then – but we'll let them off), more often than not, when it comes to picking the best, you're at the mercy of lady luck on the night.

■ ■ ■ Italian

■ ■ ■ Croma
Clarence Street, off Albert Square
(0161) 237 9799

This restaurant opened just over two years ago when two managers from Pizza Express departed to claim a slice of the Manchester pizza action for themselves (ho ho). And so Croma was born. Busy every night of the week without fail, during it's short life this restaurant has been catapulted to the elevated status of one of the places to eat in

Manchester. To be fair though, you can easily recognise the parentage – Croma has definitely inherited Pizza Express characteristics, but it's independent and unique and therefore has the edge. The atmosphere is friendly, aided by the very stylish and spacious surroundings and the service is excellent.
Mon-Sat 11-11, Sun 11-10.30
Meal for two: £22.85 (Anatra – Peking Duck Pizza)

■ ■ ■ Don Giovanni's
11 Oxford Street (0161) 228 2482

They've not gone for the modern minimalism of so many of the restaurants in Manchester – which makes for a much cosier and warmer environment, if a little cluttered. If the plaster-cast busts (thanks Mr Angelo) and draped vine leaves don't transport you as if by magic into the heart of Venice, then the food may stand a better chance. Damn tasty dishes that certainly won't leave you hungry, attentive service and a wide choice of wines all combine to make this a very pleasant evening out indeed. Don't expect to be able to go out dancing afterwards – this is a restaurant to go to when the meal is your evening out.
Tue-Sun 12-2.30, Mon-Thu 5-11, Fri-Sat 5-11.30, Sun 5-10.30
Meal for two: £30.40 (Chicken Tricoli)

◼◼◼ Caffé Uno

**Albert Square (0161) 834 7633
651 Wilmslow Road, Didsbury
(0161) 448 0888**

A refurb and a grand opening later, both these branches are much the same – perfect for those 'ad-hoc kind of can't be bothered to cook so let's eat out' kind of moments. Food's pretty decent and the prices aren't much to complain about either. The Albert Square branch definitely has the best setting. With European style pavement seating overlooking the Town Hall - eh, now that's civilised innit?

*Mon-Thu 10-10.30, Fri-Sat 10-12,
Sun 11-10pm*
Meal for two: £24.40 (Gnocchi Modena)

◼◼◼ Cocotoo's

57 Whitworth Street (0161) 237 5458

A little piece of Italy built into a British Rail viaduct. The curved ceiling boasts a frescoed replica of the Sistine Chapel Ceiling and the waiters are so Italian you almost expect the mafia to come bursting through the doors in a gun-blazing massacre. Maybe. The prices are very reasonable considering the decadent surroundings – around £12 per head for a three-course meal. The wines range from £10.90 for the house selection to £34.80 top price. Of course, all of Italy is represented here, from pastas and risottos to tiramisu, and even some traditional irritating arrogance in the service. A 'we don't need your custom' attitude means you feel like they're doing you a favour even letting you have a table, let alone getting you a glass of water. Sort it out hey?

Mon-Sat 12-2.30, 5.30-11.15
Meal for two: £23.40 (any pizza)

■ ■ Pizza Express

95 Lapwing Lane, West Didsbury
(0161) 438 0838
6 South King Street (0161) 834 0145
56 Peter Street (0161) 839 9300
The Triangle (0161) 834 6130

It's official – Pizza Express has actually bought Manchester. More prolific in the city now than McDonalds – you've got a whopping four to choose from. The menu's are all the same – you've probably already got your Pizza Express favourite. All the pizzas are delicious (if slightly on the small side) and the dough balls are the stuff of legends. This chain certainly knows how to pick lovely buildings and perfect locations – from the old high-vaulted ceilings of the West Didsbury branch, to the modern clean lines of the King Street one. It's one of those places you can always rely on to deliver – and there isn't a bad one out of any of these. Though if you're in a rush I'd go to the Peter Street branch as that tends to be the quietest.
Mon-Sat 11.30-12am, Sun 12-11.30
Meal for two: £23.75 (Fiorentina Pizza)

■ ■ Palmiro

197 Upper Chorlton Street
(0161) 860 7330

A splendid little independent restaurant that's well worth seeking out. Open for a year now and run by a friendly couple Stefano and Julie, Palmiro is proving to be one of the most respected and authentic Italian restaurants in Manchester. The dishes are honest and are all regional Italian recipes – food that Italians really eat, which makes a change. The décor is brutally, but refreshingly, minimalist – with clichés such as watercolours of Venice mercifully omitted from the walls. Trendies, foodies, media types and the Cheshire set all flock here on a regular basis. The quality of the ingredients is never compromised and the restaurant often busy; it's safe to say that Palmiro has a very promising future.
Tue-Sun 6-10.30; also open for Sunday brunch 11-3pm
Meal for two: £31.25 (Rib Eye Steak) menu changes every 4-6 weeks

■ ■ Japanese

■ ■ Wagamamas

The Printworks (0161) 839 5916

Proof that fast food can taste good. You arrive, you're seated, your order is taken straight away, and your food arrives within 10 minutes, piping hot and bloody beautiful. Wagamamas is all about looking after yourself through positive eating and positive living. We realise this sounds painfully trite/shite, but bear with us. You can start by ordering yourself one of their fruit juices (for general cleaning and digestion). Follow that with some gyoza (chicken dumplings to you and me) and some ramen (Chinese-style thread noodles) or any other of their generous main dishes, and you're on your way to being a very healthy bunny indeed. There you go. And obviously, it's entirely no-smoking. Personally, I'd sooner run naked through a field of nettles than compromise health over substance, but there are clearly some freaks who enjoy this kind of thing.

Mon-Sat 12-11, Sun 12.30-10
Meal for two: £19.20 (Yaki Soba – stir fry noodles with chicken and prawns)

■■■ Tampopo
16 Albert Square (0161) 819 1966

Situated on Albert Square, this is a Manchester stalwart. If you haven't been here already – go, immediately. Tampopo serves excellent food, that should be enough reason alone – but combine this with efficient and friendly service, a modern, clean, and sociable environment and very reasonable prices… and you end up with the perfect city centre restaurant. Post-work, pre-theatre, mid way through a bar crawl – a favourite with the itchy team, and with half of the population of Manchester.

Mon-Sat 12-11, Sun 12-10pm
Meal for two: £22.25 (Padthai Noodles)

■■■ Thai

■■■ Lemongrass
Copson Street, Withington (0161)434 2345

Take a stroll down Withington High Street and you might not associate the local 'hood as supporting one of the finest restaurants in the city. Yet take the turning onto Copson Street by Cinecity and uncover the culinary delights of Lemongrass restaurant. OK, there's the ominously required knock on the door to gain entrance, but it's all part of the experience. The décor is not much to shout about (though the ceiling is pretty cool) as they let the food do the talking at this authentic Thai restaurant. A massive menu is on offer with

Ruth, 20, Business student

Drinking – do you go for hardcore binges or lightweight supping?
I go to Loaf or Revolution, so supping I guess
And lightweight clubbing too then?
Uh... Paradise, so not exactly lightweight
Bet you eat salads and healthy stuff
The café bars serve good food, yes.
And your threads?
High Street places for the most part
Best thing about Manchester?
Lots of students and everywhere's always busy
I said the best. And the worst?
Not enough diversity of music – no R&B or Hip Hop

specialist noodle recipes and golden rice dishes costing between £7-£12. The food is fantastic and plentiful and it's ideal for taking your nearest and dearest for some candlelit ambiance. Highly recommended, but remember to bring your own booze.
Mon-Thu 6.30-10, Fri-Sat 9.30-late, Sun 7-9.15
Meal for two: £13 (Thai Green Curry)

■ ■ ■ Thai-E-Sarn
Burton Road, W Didsbury (0161) 445 5200
What a gem this is. You simply have to visit for two very good reasons. The first, and most important, is the food. A truly excellent, very extensive menu, all of which is lovingly prepared. The second reason is that the manageress, the lovely but eccentric Wendy, makes this an eating experience to remember. If she's not singing already – then do ask her to, and she'll be more than happy to oblige. With karaoke tapes which cover the entire careers of both Elvis and Shirley Bassey – she'll get you singing along whether you like it or not. You have to join in this particularly warm, fun and friendly restaurant.
Tue-Fri 12-2, Mon-Sun 6-11.30
Meal for two: £21.95 (Thai Green Curry)

■ ■ ■ Vegetarian

■ ■ ■ Greens
Lapwing Lane, West Didsbury
(0161) 434 4259
This is the ultimate veggie restaurant. The food is absolutely delicious – even the biggest carnivores won't miss the meat – and the set menus are great value for money. To make for an even cheaper night out its BYO, but remember to book in advance – it's

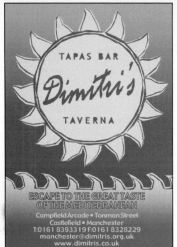

only about 20 people can fit in at one time (including the two people cooking and serving the food). Set back away from the mini-Blackpool-style neon that is Rusholme at night, and catering for veggies, vegans, and people who have grown out of the 'I don't like vegetables' age – this restaurant serves literally hundreds of dishes without feeling the need to throw a dead animal into the pot. In order to really make its mark on the food map and before it can be considered as a serious contender for a pleasant meal, it needs cleaning up, both inside and out.
12-late (they only chuck you out when you've finished)
Meal for two: £24.90 (Szechwan Style Egg Plant + litre of wine)

■ ■ ■ Others

■ ■ ■ BED
Under Tribeca, Sackville Street (0161) 236 8300

a tiny place and its almost always busy – Greens has built up such a reputation for itself that people travel from all across Manchester to eat here, and rightly so too.
Mon, Sat 5.30-10.30, Tue-Fri 12-2, 5.30-10.30, Sun 12-2.30, 5.30-10.30
Set menu – £5 lunch time (2 courses); £10 dinner (2 courses – additional starter/dessert £2.50)

■ ■ ■ The Greenhouse
331 Great Western Street (0161) 224 0730
A quirky little restaurant. Quirky in that it looks like it should have been certified as a dangerous building years ago. Little in that

Dark and dimly lit, this small basement restaurant is just a little bit different. There are tables available for the conventional amongst you – but lets talk a bit more about the beds, because that's what it's really all about. They're thankfully not all that squishy – but still very comfortable. Kick off your shoes (pray to God that your dining partner doesn't have foot odour problems) and lie back. Each bed is separated by a net curtain – you eat off your knee and drinks are propped precariously on trays on the bed. If you start feeling a little more sociable, pull

SO DON'T APPLY FOR IT.

back the curtain and do a bit of bed-hopping. Very relaxed and different – and the food's pretty tasty too. I've also thankfully managed to write the review without it becoming a pun-o-rama, but can't resist saying – come on kids, it's time for BED.

Tue-Sat 7-2am
Meal for two: £33.55 (Alligator sweet spiced with flash fries)

■ ■ ■ Dimitri's
Campfield Arcade, Deansgate
(0161) 839 3319

A lively and friendly restaurant at the Castlefield end of Deansgate, Dimitris is very popular indeed. There's sheltered outdoor seating in the alley at the back – and the place has an authenticity that's guaranteed to spirit you straight back to your favourite taverna from last years holiday in Corfu. With live music in the front bar, where you're more than welcome to pop in just for a drink – it's a knees-up everyone's-smiling kind of place. Get into the spirit of Dimitri's by consuming at least a carraffe of wine each – absolutely everyone's pissed up, including half the staff.

Mon-Thu 11-12, Fri & Sat 11-1, Sun 11-11
Meal for two: £30.85 (Rosto)

■ ■ ■ Dutch Pancake House
Oxford Street (0161) 228 1851

Its cheap, so why am I not cheerful? A child-friendly (not looking good then), pretty tatty, simplistic restaurant. More of a café than an à la carte, it's reminiscent of the kind of eatery that's normally found at a second-rate theme park – wipe clean tables, massive tasteless portions and glasses of flat coke. One thing you may gain from an experience in this shabby dungeon of Oxford Street is the realisation of why pancakes are generally only recommended one day of the year.

Mon-Sat 12-10.30, Sun 12-7.30
Meal for two: £12 (Savoury Pancake with Ham)

■ ■ ■ Gaucho Grill
2a St Marys Street (0161) 833 4333

In case you're wondering the name 'Gaucho Grill' comes from the original Argentinean cowboy, (or 'Gaucho'), tradition of cooking big juicy meats over huge wooden fires. That's enough history for now children, all you need to know is that The Gaucho Grill is a restaurant of Argentinean leanings, and

there's a mighty fine range of steaks and sausages to be found there. The menu is predominantly for meat-eaters, although there are veggie options and certain dishes can be made to suit dietary requirements. Big main meals include corn fed chicken (£9.50), calf's liver (ewwww, £11.00) and the organic steak dishes (from £9.00), all of which can be served with different sauces and side orders.

Mon-Sat 12-12, Sun 12-10.30
Meal for two: £47.50 (Biggest Argentinian Steaks)

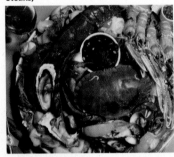

■■■ Livebait
Lloyd Street, Albert Square
(0161) 817 4110

Oh God, I hope not. I know they don't have feelings but we're not eating them live now surely? This is a fine example of a seafood restaurant. For those who reckon the only thing that Manchester is missing is a beach – Livebait is as close as you'll get to an authentic sea-front restaurant. You've guessed it – the theme here is fish, crabs, muscles and so on, all dished up in a variety of ways to a wide range of customers. Popular pre-theatre and steadily busy throughout the week, it's well worth a visit for something a bit different.

Mon-Wed 12-11, Thu-Sat 12-12
Meal for two: £31.00 (Shellfish Platter)

■■■ Mongolian Barbecue
Chorlton Street (0161) 228 1631

This one's definitely a place for big groups and celebrations rather than an intimate meal for two. Far too much audience participation for my liking – I wanna be looked after, but here you have to choose your own food (by filling a bowl full of whatever you fancy from the wide range of fresh ingredients), stand in a queue, watch it get cooked and then take it back to your table. OK, so I am lazy – everyone else seemed to be having a good time, and those chefs are pretty clever with their giant chopstick thingy whatsits.

Mon-Thu 6-10.30, Fri 6-11, Sat 1-11,
Sun 1-10.30. Meal for two: £31.85
(Mongolian BBQ – all you can eat)

■■■ PerSia
1 Great Northern, Deansgate
(0161) 839 4889

This is a classy five-star eating experience. Thoroughly splendid in every way – the décor (though not entirely authentic) is thoughtfully reminiscent of the richness of the Far East, with this vast space adorned with chandeliers, rugs, yellow walls, pillars and balconies. The wine list is extensive, the service outstanding (nothing is too much trouble) and the food simply delicious. For an added bonus PerSia really comes to life at the weekends or on special occasions, with belly dancers, snake charmers and live music. A very colourful and enjoyable night out – shame you have to step out onto rainy Peter Street or Deansgate at the end of the evening rather than on to warm sands…

Mon-Sat 8am-3am (last food orders at 12am), Sun 11am-2am
Meal for two: £36.50 (Fish Kebab)

■ ■ ■ Piranha
27 Sackville Street (0161) 288 7800

What was once Lush is now Piranha, but it's still as Lush as ever. The space itself is lovely – open, fresh, clean and stylish, with the glass staircase still dominating the entrance. Whether visited as a bar or a restaurant, Piranha in its first few months has a certain buzz to it, and serves up some tasty dishes and a good selection of wines and spirits. The service is very genial and helpful. There's also always a good selection of fit and good looking, smartly dressed customers wandering around, though try not to let your date notice you looking.

Mon-Sat 5-11, Sun 1-10.30
Meal for two: £29 (Red Snapper Fillet)
HH: 5-8pm when HW is £8

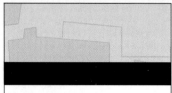
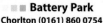

cafés

www.itchymanchester.co.uk

■ ■ ■ Battery Park
Chorlton (0161) 860 0754

The original juice bar (and still the only one in South Manchester), Battery Park has fooled many a thirsty punter stumbling in looking for pints. It's just juice, that's it, no matter how politely you ask. Fresh juice mind, freshly squeezed, together with shakes and a fine range of coffees and herbal teas - and it's all very tasty (even the ones with proper revitalising ingredients such as ginseng). May not be able to cure the shakes, but might help you shake off a hangover.

Mon-Fri 9-6pm, Sat 10-6pm, Sun 11-5pm
Mozzerella Ciabatta £2.75 (eat in)

■ ■ ■ Café Mitre
Cathedral Gates (0161) 834 4128

This is such a hidden gem we're almost loathed to tell anyone about it, but here goes. Outside you've got M&S, The Triangle, The Printworks, screaming babies, bustling shoppers and irritating skateboarders. Inside you have tea for two, buttered crumpets, old people and a chaise longue. Café Mitre is a seaside café smack bang in the heart of Manchester. It's never busy, it's never noisy, and it never fails to deliver. The sandwiches come cut into triangles with big hearty chips and a fruity salad, the cakes are fresh and juicy, the sugar comes in cubes and the service comes with a smile. Lovely.

Mon closed, Tue–Sat 11-4pm, Sun 12-5pm
Ham and Mustard sandwich with salad and chips £3.25

■■ Café Pop
Oldham Street (0161) 237 9688

The Northern Quarter is a little on the grey side. It's not the most cheerful or polished of places, and with the all-too-cool moodiness of the arty types reading books and sulking about the place, it can all get a little depressing. Then there's the beckon of kitsch that is Café Pop. Garish colours and cluttered walls surround curvy tables and chairs and menus wrapped around tins – it's all so bloody cheerful, and refreshing it is too. The food is all lovingly prepared in the tiny kitchen at the back (some things better than others – you might be wise to stick to the salad selection, which is always good). The freshly made fruit milkshakes are a must.

Mon-Thu 9.30-5.30, Fri-Sat 9.30-7, Sun 10am-5pm
Full Vegetarian Breakfast £3.90

■■ The Craft Centre
17 Oak Street (0161) 832 1515

Sit under the huge paper maché cow and gaze knowledgably at the art surrounding you. Top-notch snacks, lunches, breakfasts and coffees. Do a bit of ear-wigging and you'll probably overhear the next Damien Hirst discussing the merits of their work, or an A&R from one of the nearby labels signing the next big thing.

Mon-Sat 10am-5.30pm
Chicken, Bacon & Avacado on choice of breads and massive salad £2.50

■■ Fletcher Moss Park Café
Wilmslow Road, Didsbury (0161) 445 4241

This little beauty can be found within the old buildings just above the botanical gar-

dens at the Fletcher Moss Park. You'll know you're drawing close to the café as the numbers of old women scattered about increases - sitting in coats and hats midsummer commenting on how delicious their ice-cream cone is. Within the café itself are just a few tables and seats, but everything on offer in here has an authentic homemade feel to it. Delicious cakes and a proper cup of tea. Opening times are the same as the parks (pretty hit and miss in the winter months).

■ ■ Love Saves The Day
Tib Street (0161) 832 0777

The jewel in the Northern Quarter crown and no mistake. Super trendy coffee shop-cum-deli-cum-supermarket for musos, hippies, teachers, media folk and the like. They make and sell their own coffee, and very good it is too, but if you fancy a bit more than a quick caffeine rush, then there's cakes and pastries, fancy sarnies and snacks, moving on to the deli counter, there are cheeses and olives and dips and free tasting opportunities. The supermarket isn't your loaf of bread and a pint of milk kind of place, it's more for those imported goods, beautifully bottled green tea, American preserves in kitsch packaging, which either has you creaming your tea or getting your goat. It's not cheap, but then remember, neither are you.

9.30am-7pm Mon-Sat
House Salad (changed daily) £4.90

■ ■ The Okassional Café

A philosophy of café culture currently enjoying its seventh location. Formerly located on the Kro Bar premises, it built a legendary reputation amongst students and clubbers by playing host to all night parties. Currently

it can be found at 62 Charles Street in between Po Na Na and HSBC bank. It acts as a meeting point for like-minded people: clubbers, activists, and all types of groups meet here for plenty of lively discussion. The café only serves fair trade dishes so if you like a full-cream coffee made by starving kids on pitiful wages, then you may have to look elsewhere. A donation of about 50p is requested for a cup and you can have soya milk. At the time of writing there's no alcohol served and no news of how long it will remain where it is but if you want to experience authentic Manchester counterculture...look no further.

■ ■ On The 8th Day
107-111 Oxford Road (0161) 273 4878

This is the student's favourite when it comes to good honest vegetarian home cooking. The menu changes every day, with veggie and vegan options only. There's always some hot goods knocking about, like mushroom stroganoff, vegetable Dhansak and hot sausage baguettes. Or, you can pile high a bowl full of fancy salad stuffs – bean sprouts, chickpeas, seasoned potato salad etc. Fluid wise, they're big on juices and smoothies. You get massive portions for a reasonable price, without scrimping on quality and taste. They've even got their own shop next door that sells over 800 organic products, candles, crystals and other soothing artefacts. Yeah man.

Mon-Fri 9am-7pm, Sat 10am-4pm
Vegan Stew (varies daily) £2.60

Internet Cafes

Easy Everything
St Annes Sq (0161) 832 9200

This place is open 24-7. And people, it's a colossus. 375 computers available to surf the net at any time of day – you'd think it was a cross between a call centre and a porn empire – but no. Easy to afford, easy to use, easy to find a free machine, and easy to get kicked out if you try to by-pass security and download porn. Apparently, trade picks up between 5-8am when some pretty odd office types go to town to surf the net before work – and there's me thinking that's what everyone does at work all day anyway.

Café closes at 2am and re-opens at 7am
Hot Chicken Salsa Sandwich with Coffee Latte £3.99
£1 buys you between 40mins and 4hours depending on time of day.

Internet Xchange
Above Coffee Republic, Piccadilly (0161) 833 3111

The Internet Xchange is a separate company from Coffee Republic, but doesn't sell it's own food and snacks – so you'll have to purchase them from downstairs (which they're quite happy for you to take up and consume whilst you compute). I've seen two people go arse over tit in a quite humiliating (and painful) fashion doing this though – so watch your step up those stairs.

Mon-Fri 7.30-6.30, Sat 8-6.30, Sun 9-5.30
Members £2 per hour, non-members £4 per hour.

top 5	BACARDI BREEZER
in association with	

Cafes

1. The Craft Centre
2. Battery Park
3. Love Saves The Day
4. Cafe Pop
5. John Dalton Cafe

Interc@fe
Debenhams, Market Street (0161) 838 8529

Situated inside one of the blandest and most boring department stores I've ever had the misfortune to get lost in, this is probably one of the most bland and boring internet cafes too – but hell, that depends which sites you visit I 'spose. 12 computers could mean a wait, but rarely does, as it's not the cheapest surfing space in the city.

Mon-Sat 10-6m, except Thu 9-8
Tuna Ciabatta with Coffee Latte £4.20
£1.50 per half hour

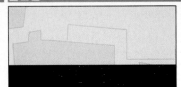

www.itchymanchester.co.uk

Meal for two prices; we've doubled the cost of a main meal and added on a bottle of the skanky house wine, so actual price of a meal may vary.

■ ■ Manchester City Centre

Don your urban street gear from Arc, toke a quick 'cigarette' whilst walking to the bus stop and casually roll up at one of the bars on Oldham Street. Or shoehorn yourself into two sizes too small leather and sequin affairs and dive head first into the glamour that is Deansgate Locks at the weekend. Whatever you're into, you'll find a spiritual home in at least one of the numerous, diverse, and rather excellent cafés and bars in Manchester's city centre.

■ ■ City Centre: Castlefield / Deansgate Locks

■ ■ Aqua
14 Albion Street (0161) 228 1800

Who let the dogs out? And the staff, and the punters for that matter. They all scarpered to a multitude of other bars in Deansgate Locks about 18 months ago, leaving nothing behind but a bunch of cast-off battered furniture. But it shouldn't really be like this – what, with a fine location by the canal and a spacious main bar? We think they've got the hint now, and they're bouncing back with a number of new weekend nights, such as Airport Lounge (mix of funk, Latino sounds, free food and presumably endless delays), together with a multitude of drinks offers. We reckon they can do it, but only the punters can decide.

Sun-Mon closed, Fri/Sat 4pm-1.30am

FAR EAST
MASSAGE
PARLOUR

·····THE JK AND JOEL BREAKFAST SHOW··········
··WHAT ARE YOU GETTING UP TO?···

BAA Manchester
Whitworth Street
Deansgate Locks Manchester
www.baabar.co.uk

■ ■ Atlas
Deansgate (0161) 834 2124

When the meedja crowd finish their mind-bendingly weighty jobs, like writing press releases for corn snacks, greeting D-list celebrities, oh and writing reviews for bars and clubs, they unwind at Atlas for a feast of imported beers and root vegetable crisps and houmous. It is quite pricey, but it's perfect for long summer evenings, never too busy and features some stunning interiors and a beautifully crafted beer garden. Food comes courtesy of the deli 'round the corner where you can feast on standard issue fashionably fancy fodder

Mon-Sat 11-11pm, Sun 11-10.30pm
Meal for two: £20 (Fish Soup)

■ ■ Baa Bar
Deansgate Locks (0161) 832 4446

For Deansgate Lock posers who can't be arsed ageing in the queue for Loaf, Baa Bar is a shiny refuge. Hideously cool, from the Tetris-shaped couches that mean you can only talk to one of your friends at a time to the vast array of glitterballs that adorn the ceiling and the airport arrivals styled drinks menu board above the bar. Best of all, handy vertical windows from the unisex toilets mean the casual urinator can peer out over the festivities. Another room is to open by the time we go to press; surely worth checking out but can discoland handle any more glitterball action?

Mon-Sat 5pm-2am. Closed Sun

itchy sms @
www.itchymanchester.co.uk

wine with lunch
with this TVT

■ ■ ■ Barça

Arches 8/9 Catalan Square, Castlefield
(0161) 839 7099

The flame-haired crooner that is Mick Hucknall has something to do with it – no one's really sure what - but Barça is more than a wannabes drinking hole. The restaurant is lovely, and sitting outside on a balmy summer evening is lush (they've also got a VIP balcony, upon which you can often spot the odd celebrity – though they get upset if you call them odd). Although I can't stand being surrounded by blonde stick insects with big boobs, and perma-tanned sales execs with gelled hair and bad shoes... I still end up in Barca all too often when the weather's good.

Mon-Thu 11-12, Fri-Sat 11-2am,
Sun 11-10.30pm.
Meal for two: £45.85 (Steak Fillet)

■ ■ ■ Fat Cat

Arch 8 Deansgate Locks (0161) 839 8243

When this bar first sprung up it just seemed to be more of the same along the Deansgate Locks row, but when it comes to lunches, music policy and atmosphere, it blows the competition out of the water. The highlight is Sunday roast, cooked better than your mum ever could (I just know, alright?), with perfect roast potatoes, melt-in-the-mouth chicken, and crispy Yorkshire puds – all reasonably priced. As a bar, Fat Cat often has live music, ranging from jazz to indie, it also hosts Afficionado on Sunday nights where you can catch the likes of Unabombers, Mark Rae, (of him and Christian fame) and Mr Scruff – very credible indeed.

Wed-Sat; 10-2am Sun 10-12am
Meal for two: £21.35 (Sunday Roast)

Carolina, 21, Shop assistant

You're from Barcelona. Without confounding stereotypes, where do you drink?
La Tasca
And then swivel your hips?
Copacabana
What kind of food do you like
The kind you can buy in La Tasca
Any great British shops take your fancy? I go to Jigsaw, Zara, Mango
But, but, what brought you here?
The shopping's great
And what'd drive you away?
The weather – I hate it

■ ■ Loaf

Deansgate Locks (0161) 819 5858

"I say, I mean, darling, just look at those beautiful curved ceilings, and the chasm of space created by the viaduct, and oh, the wall of mirrors is simply gorgeous. I mean, who cares about prices when the place is just ... just so me". Uh, yeah. Incredibly popular, seeing long tailing queues at weekends, this gleaming bar is both brilliant and appalling in equal measures. Table service always goes down a treat, and the crowd is strictly beautiful, with a door policy to enforce it. Sometimes though, in and

amongst all the glitterati you wonder if everyone's not more obsessed with image than conversation. The monkeys.
Sun-Wed 12-12.30, Thu-Sat 12-2am
Meal for two: £25 (Mushroom Risotto)

■ ■ ■ The Lock

Deansgate Locks (0161) 833 4222

With a cool million to play with, the Lock crew have come up with a sumptuous restaurant/bar and coffee shop combo, with a 'members only' mezzanine thrown in for extra snooty measure. The food, tasty as it is, is way overpriced, ditto for the drinks, the sandwiches and the coffees. Downstairs dining offers the alfresco option by the water –

nice in theory, but do you really want to be up close and personal with the Manchester Ship canal? The Lock never seems to be anything like as busy as the neighbouring bars – which may well be a good thing if you're dodging the masses, but obviously isn't the way they want it. It's all very expensive and

!	☐	✏	From	Subject
!	✉		itchycity.co.uk	Restaurant recommendations via e-mail

posh looking so it'll probably suit you down to the ground if you're very expensive and, er, posh looking.

Mon-Wed 11-12.30am, Thu-Sat 11-2am,
Sun 11-10.30pm
Meal for two: £41.95 (Venison Scallops)
HH: 4-7pm Mon-Fri - 2 4 1 on cocktails.

◻ ■ ■ Revolution
Wilmslow Road, Fallowfield
(0161) 225 7529
Deansgate Locks (0161) 839 7569
88 Oxford Street (0161) 237 5377

You say you want a revolution? Well you know, Manchester's got three. And they're all fine bars indeed. They're not going to save the world, but when it comes to having some good daytime grub, or spending the night getting vodka'd up and getting down, you can count us in. This successful chain started in Manchester and has now not only

spread over this city, but indeed the whole country like a rash. The most committed bars remain at the roots of the uprising though, with the one in Fallowfield being largely student dominated, the one on Oxford Street remaining a popular stalwart for the BBC and Uni crew and the newer, massive swanky Deansgate Locks version mad busy at the weekend. All three offer the awe-inspiring range of vodkas we've come to expect, as well as loud music and a young up-for-it clientele.

Opening times vary
Meal for two: £17 (Fireman Steak)

■ ■ City Centre: Northern Quarter

◻ ■ ■ Bar Code
Oldham Street (0161) 236 0029

This place used to be called Squizzy Taylors – aka scally-central. And it's owned by the same folk who gave us the inexcusably bad Idols across the road. So it's got to come as a surprise that they've done a respectable job on Bar Code; out went the tools and spanners, in came a stock of comfy, classy leather sofas and modern art. Refreshingly, they charge a mere £1.70 a pint, making it one of the better-value joints in the Northern Quarter. Taking it on face value, you might just grow to love this hidden gem. Also, watch out for the three kitchen hands chain-smoking at the end of the bar, passing comment on everyone.

Mon-Sat 11.30am-11pm, Sun 12-6pm
Meal for two: £16 (Lasagne & Garlic Bread)
HH: 11.30-7pm doubles for price of singles

✳ KEY103 **feel the noise**

DRY**201**

The Original Café Bar

28-30 oldham street manchester
t 0161 236 9840
e info@drybar.co.uk
www.drybar.co.uk

■ ■ ■ Dry 201

Oldham Street (0161) 236 9840

Dry Bar's reputation goes before it; this is as much a part of Manchester as the Ship Canal. The bar that used to be known as Fac 201 (as in Factory Records), opened up in

1990, and was pre-club action to the Hacienda, creating with it a sense of style and occasion to the lively but then unattractive Oldham Street. The Haç died but Fac lived on – now known as Dry 201 – and its lived-in cool now fights off competition from all the newcomers in town. With a good selection of beers and spirits (the happy hour offering pints for £1.50 and wine for £1.30) and great food provided by Dr Livvy's kitchen, Dry is the place to unwind after a hard day's night.

Mon/Tue 11-11pm, Wed-Sat 11-2am, Sun 12-10.30pm.
Meal for two: £15 (Chicken Burger).
HH: 4-9pm Mon-Fri, all day Sun

■ ■ ■ Cord Bar

Off Tib Street (0161) 832 9494

It's only been open a short while but already it's practically a members' club for the musicians, record labels, DJs and production folk of Manchester. This means you can (we do anyway), feel a tad un-cool unless these are your people. The grub is kept simple – quiche when it's hot, stew when it's not. The name's inspired by corduroy, to which the décor also pays homage with the upholstery and wall panels. Don't make the mistake of fiddling with the wooden fixtures at the side of the tables – when we say 'fixtures' we're using the term loosely. And so are they. Incidentally, well worth a visit is the monthly pub quiz, clearly the stuff of lucid drug-fuelled day-dreams. All the losing teams for each round take it in turns to spin the wheel of misfortune, with forfeits ranging from snogging Elsie the bemused dog to snorting vodka.

Mon-Sat 12-11pm, Sun 12-10.30pm
Meal for two: £20.20 (Stew)

■ ■ ■ Centro
72-74 Tib Street (0161) 835 2863

Eddie Izzard once said there's a full fashion circle going round from being cool, getting cooler, cool as you please and looking like a wanker. Centro falls precariously in between the two extremes, with a crowd dressed in Twisted Nerve clothing with beards or cute plaits, armed with an obligatory copy of Sleaze Nation. It's not that big, or mightily impressive, but it does have kudos. And Leffe beer.

Mon-Thu 12-12, Fri-Sat 12-1am, Closed Sun
Meal for two: £13.40 (Hot chicken baguette)

■ ■ ■ Night & Day
26 Oldham Street (0161) 236 4597

Unlike the eye-poppingly bright Nite and Day convenience stores, this bar is damn dingy. And even if you love dingy, it's a shade darker. As such, it's become a haven for musos, musicians and grebos, drawn to the lack of light, the daytime food and the multitude of bands that rock up in the evening. Come in for a quick one, and before you know it, it's way past your bedtime, the frozen margaritas and Jaegermeisters have taken hold and you're talking to a man who knew a dog who lived near Mark E Smith.

Mon-Sat 11-2am
Meal for two: £17.30 (Cajun Chicken)

■ ■ ■ City Centre:
Peter Street / Deansgate

■ ■ ■ Life Café
Peter Street (0161) 833 3000

Life Café in Liverpool has a very glamorous reputation - it's where the cast and crew of Brookie and Hollyoaks like to mingle with the general public. A pub/club/restaurant rolled into one, and a right posh affair by all accounts. Life Café Manchester is sadly not as exciting (although the food comes served on sizzling plates spitting hot oil at you - which livens the evening up no end). Don't write it off completely though, as it does play host to some decent live music, and to be fair the food ain't half bad, while the service is un-nervingly friendly and efficient.

Mon-Tues 12-11pm, Wed-Sat 12-2am
Meal for two: £26.85 (Corn Fed Chicken)

■ ■ ■ RSVP
Deansgate (0161) 839 0985

"Right lads, our pubs are taking a pounding from these new-fangled bars, so what are we going to do? Give me a name that sounds cultured. RSVP? That'll do. Now, wooden floors, naturally, lots of seating – the girls love it – bit of chrome around the place and bish bash bosh, we've a winner on our hands". Except it's not; this place is entirely unremarkable.

Mon-Thu 9am-11pm, Fri 9-2am, Sat 12-2am, Sun 12-10.30pm
Meal for two: £17.90 (Thai Chicken Sarny)
HH: Wine £5 per bottle on Tues ; 5-7pm everyday - cocktails £2.75

! 🗋 ⌗	From	Subject
! ✉	itchycity.co.uk	Drinks deals via e-mail

maintain their position on the very lowest rung of the evolutionary ladder. Oh please, dear Lord, don't tell me I have to ever go there again, I still have nightmares.
Mon-Sat 4pm-2am, closed Sunday
No food. HW: £9.50
HH: Mon-Thu 7-9pm - 2 4 1 all drinks

■■■ Soft
Peter Street (0161) 839 6263

...as shite, the crowd most certainly aren't. It's a pack them in, knock 'em back and get clattered type affair. Pre-club boozing without much sophistication, but with plenty of drinks offers and commercial tunes as loved by the Peter Street posse. Formerly Joup bar, big and clever it clearly isn't, but they never intended it that way. Around 12.30am people tend to slope off to the clubs and there's much more room to chill-out if you want to shun the crowds.
Mon-Fri 5pm-2am, Sat 8pm-2am, closed Sun
No food HW: £8
HH: 5-8pm, 2-4-1 on everything.

■■■ Teasers
Deansgate (0161) 833 3118

Tease us - you've got to be joking? Bad, bad, bad. It may look like a tacky but "if you forget where you are it's kind of OK type place", but oh no, it really is the arse end of the universe. Babes 'n' Beer - legwarmers, hot-pants, high-kicks and high-jinks – all encapsulated in an Americanised arch of The Great Northern redevelopment. The male half (ok, so they probably represent slightly more than half) of the clientele in here are struggling to

■■■ Norwegian Blue
The Printworks (0161) 839 1451

Home to the youngest-looking 18-year olds we've ever seen, Norwegian Blue is a youngster's cocktail-tastic chart-fest for those devoid of any taste or sense. There's plenty to be upset about for any discerning customer – the long queues at the bar, the unbearably loud pop music, the plethora of spotty, townie drunks, and the disappointment of the 'cascading 30 foot high waterfall behind the bar' (you've just gotta see it for yourself to believe how unimpressive it is in the flesh). You'll enjoy this bar a lot more if you go when their regular customers are watching Shrek at the cinema, as when it's

itchy sms @
www.itchymanchester.co.uk

quiet the food's pretty decent and the service is much quicker.

Mon-Thu 10am-12am, Fri-Sat 10-2am, Sun 12-10.30pm
Meal for two: £22.85 (Gambalaia -Cajun Sausage Stew)

■ ■ Tiger Tiger
The Printworks (0161) 385 8080

Are they drawing parallels with Blake's famous masterpiece? Well it does burn 'bright' and it all happens at 'night' but is it good or is it…not? Well that depends on your level of corporate dronery. Because this isn't a masterpiece; it's a master-plan. Once you're in its jaws you're never meant to leave. And, for a mediocre night out, you won't have to. It's a multi-storey megablock of over-priced restaurants, clubs and bars, the many coffers of which filter down to make our clever cat grow very fat indeed. So drones: dress up, line up, then cough up – the Tiger's really hungry.

Mon-Sat 12-2am, Sun 12-12.30am
Mixture of café bar and restaurant food in the different areas – prices vary

■ ■ Zinc
The Triangle (0161) 827 4200

A year 2002 café bar experience if ever there was one – a schmooth cocktail of slick service, stylish surroundings, excellent food, funky music (supplied by the likes of the Unabombers and Paper Recordings), and a young-but-affluent style-conscious crowd. Popular, but not so much that you're squeezed in between a well-perfumed armpit and a deconstructed-chic covered rear-end – there's plenty of room to admire the good-looking clientele. Some places have it and some places don't – and Zinc's definitely got it. Intriguingly, amidst all the interior design high-points they've decided to give us all some exercise by situating the toilets down a corridor so long it brings you out in a bunker under Ancotes - nice touch.

Mon-Thu 10-12am, Fri-Sat 10-2am, Sun 12-10.30pm
Meal for two: £29.50 (Marinated Lamb)

LOOK AT HIM, POMPOUS IDIOT.

■ ■ City Centre: Other locations

■ ■ Citrus
Mount Street (0161) 834 1344

Watch in amazement as the office workers run faster than they've ever moved their sedentary arses, before steaming into the downstairs disco and happy hour on a Friday night as if their email connections depended on it. It gets very busy, very sweaty and very drunk and lairy. On the flip side, there's an airy and bright eatery on the top floor with an altogether more civilised/boring vibe. Take your pick...
Mon-Thu 11-11pm, Fri-Sat 11-2am, closed Sunday.
Meal for two: £27.65 (Burger with chips and salad). HH: 12-8pm Mon-Fri, cocktail HH 5-10pm Sat

■ ■ Cornerhouse Bar
70 Oxford Street (0161) 200 1508

Beard-strokers unite! At last, somewhere to scratch your hairy bush and pontificate about the latest arthouse offerings that are being shown upstairs. Musicians, artists, stu-

dents, and, frankly, lonely people all flock here for a fancy beer or a cup of Earl Grey. The cold, metal seats are a bit duff for lounging around on - probably there just to entice you into the one of their three cinema screens showing classic films. Oddly, the management refused to cooperate when asked to supply details of opening times and prices for food and drink – maybe they're planning on making the menu really pricey or something.

■ ■ Deluxe
Oxford Road (0161) 274 0607

'Artsy' in the sense that they've got ciabatta melts, Japanese beers, funky artwork, DJ workshops and glam club nights – but hey, they do it well. Strangely, not many people seem to have cottoned on to the fact that this place is actually really good – in the day to catch an actor or two studying their script, or in the evening to shake your thang and let your hair down. Weekends offer the

A MANCHESTER INSTITUTION

FAB cafe

retro arcade machines - tv / movie props - film nights
Sweets & LuckyBags - cultural & social edification
music, Booze, cigs & glamour - coolest place to hang

FREE IN til 2am

THE ULTIMATE SHARED CULTURAL EXPERIENCE 111 Portland Street · Manchester · t. 0161 236 2019

best from local DJs, with live sets from the Twisted Nerve crew and a new club night, Homodisco (offering itself as a replacement to the much lamented Homoelectric) on the horizon. Theatre bars have never felt so good.

Mon-Wed 8.30am-11pm, Thu 8.30am-2am, Fri-Sat 9am-2am.
Meal for two: £14 (Peking Duck Ciabatta).

■ ■ ■ Fab Café
Portland Street (0161) 236 2019

It's not just a bar, it's a lifestyle, don't you know? The Fab Cafe is a science fiction and cult TV theme bar, offering everything from Thunderbirds props to vintage arcade games amongst its kitsch delights. With a range of attractions, from cult film screenings to celebrity guest speakers (puppet master Gerry Anderson, papier-mache-headed 'eccentric' Frank Sidebottom), the worst that could happen on a night at the Fab Cafe is that you find yourself devoid of a chair to sit on and space to breath listening to Duran Duran's terrible cover version of 'White Lines' at ear-splitting volume. Not as bad as it sounds… apparently Johny Depp has been spotted in here four times. Fab – possibly.

Mon, Wed, Thu 4.45pm-2am, Tue 4.45-11pm, Fri-Sat 11-2am.
TV dinners served 5-7pm. HH: 5.30-7.30pm everyday, draught beer £1.50

WELL, DIGEST THIS!

■ ■ ■ Jumpin' Jaks
Portland Street (0161) 228 2036

The polar opposite to nonchalant cool, Jumpin' Jaks are a remarkable chain of bars that prove it's possible to get it wrong in one city and repeat the formula all over the country. People who've seen better days (if not decades) come here to jump, jive, sing, dance, yelp with glee – in other words make total tits out of themselves. Unpretentious, good old-fashioned fun? Actually it's just embarrassing. The staff are also forced to take part in this unadulterated merriment by dancing gaily on the bar – proving that bar jobs aren't easy money after all. You have to be a member to get in on Sundays – least said about that the better.

Mon-Wed 8pm-1am Thu-Sat 8pm-2am,
Sun 8pm–12.30am
Snacky food at the diner - Hot Dog £1.50.

■ ■ ■ Kro Bar
325 Oxford Road (0161) 274 3100

Disturbingly minimalist in decor, the Kro Bar is an unfeasibly classy alternative to the Student's Union bar. Our 'unmentionable competition' think it's pretty damn good too – voting it the Café Bar of the Year for 2001 (quite an accolade!). Whilst the clinical interior may or may not be too warm and welcoming, the heated terraces at front and back provide the perfect venue for a spot of afternoon drinking... it's bloody terrifying how little it takes to get the front patio teaming with students at the merest hint of sunshine. They spark up the barby on warm summers nights though, which makes this bar well worth a visit. Good range of imported beers too.

Mon-Fri 8.30am-11pm, Sat 10am-11pm,
Sun 10am-10.30. Meal for two: £17.50
(Full English Breakfast)

■ ■ Lime
2 Booth Street (0161) 233 2929

What ever happened to straight-forward names like 'Tap 'n' Spile', 'The Old Cock', 'The Fat Womans Arse'; all these pretentious, trendy names for bars do my 'ead in. Pretty clever to call the club under it Sublime you might think - but having visited, it just made me think of those lonely hearts ads where for 'crazy sense of humour' you should read 'civil servant that wears comedy socks'. Another formulaic Londonite addition to the Manchester scene, but at least the staff are Northern and therefore attitude-free. Contained within its citrus façade you'll discover a restaurant, a bar and a club - designed for those who want the 'all under one roof' solution to a night out.

Mon-Thu 11-11, Fri-Sat 11am-1am, Sun 11am-10.30pm
Meal for two: £41.70 (Peppered Beef Fillet)

■ ■ Sand Bar
Grovesnor Street (0161) 273 3141

You're just as likely to overhear a group of philosophy students debating the ethics of deconstruction as you are to hear media-types planning their post-production. It's a left-wing, scruffy street wear, bohemian meets media-type bar, and everyone loves it. Great tapas should be shared and washed down with any one of the 500,000 different

types of imported beers (well it feels like that many). It's the kind of bar where you always seem to manage to get the last available seat. Very relaxed and cool, and definitely worth seeking if you're out on Oxford Road.
Mon-Fri 12-11pm, Sat 5-11pm, Sun 5-10.30pm.
Menu changes regularly. HW: £6

■ ■ ■ Sofa
Wilmslow Rd, Fallowfield (0161) 248 4820
Charles Street, Centre (0161) 273 7543
In giving the Sofa brand life, Hale have transformed two of their older bars, Joshua Brooks and Shed. Now sporting stylish leather sofas, subtle colours, reading material and low coffee tables… they're bloody good looking too. By some miracle the Fallowfield one isn't totally dominated by students, despite its location directly opposite Owens Park Halls. The one on Charles Street enjoys a canal-side location and a lively pre-club atmosphere at night – the downstairs also turns into a club in its own right at the weekend. Good for drinks promotions and for catching some decent DJs doing their thing.
Fallowfield: Mon-Sat 12-11, Sun 12-10.30
Charles St: Mon 12-11, Tue-Sat 12-2am, Sun 12-10.30.
Meal for two: £14.40 (Spicy Chicken Wrap).

■ ■ ■ Tribeca
Sackville Street (0161) 236 8244
Purple – oh I think so. Think of a teenage bedroom and you're half way there (to go the whole way just pop downstairs to the restaurant). Now add huge windows along one side, a dancefloor, a long bar, DJs and loud tunes – this bar's actually pretty grown up. Tribeca's the kind of bar you go to after a hard

day at the office, or pre-clubbing. Cocktails, cheap bottles of wine in the happy hours and food that'll set you up for the evening ahead.
Mon-Sat 11am-2am
Meal for two: £30.85 (Scottish Rib-eye Steak)
HH: 4pm-7pm £5 per bottle for house wine

■ ■ ■ Withington

Withington High Street can transform a good mood into losing the will to live; it's pretty unattractive, and with its distinct lack of options it's definitely a case of quality and not quantity. So live with it.

■ ■ ■ Fuel
Wilmslow Rd, Withington (0161) 282 6040
A little purple haven. Chomp on a burrito, sup a proper cup of coffee, let your mind drift off to places far more attractive than Withington – say, Hulme. Put your feet up and relax. You're bound to feel at ease in here – it's just one of those places, unless you're allergic to students, for there are plenty of them. Fuel will certainly set you up for the day, and it isn't half bad at night either.
Mon-Sat 9am-12.30am (last food is 11.30pm), Sun everything's half hour earlier
Meal for two: £18.70 (Mexicanna Burrito with Salad and Chips)

■ ■ ■ Solomon Grundys
Wilmslow Rd, Withington (0161) 445 6722

Now we all like an experimental chef – but black soup? No wonder the woman sat behind me asked them to take it back to the kitchen and return with something that looked edible. Ah, but lets not be harsh – Solomon is seriously chilled out, and that's what makes it such a top place to sit alone and read the paper, or duck in for a quick snack in the daytime. At night it's got a good buzz about it but still remains an 'anything goes' sort of place. Some of the clientele in here are slightly *too* anything goes though – Grundy's could be called Grungy (and that's generous) as it doubles up as a drop-in centre for the local characters who'll happily adorn the bar dawn 'til dusk.
Mon-Thu 11-11pm, Fri-Sat 11-12am, Sun 11-10.30. Meal for two: £16.70 (Breakfast)

■ ■ ■ Chorlton

Chorlton is the Manchester equivalent to Camden in London: they've got the Locks, we've got The Green. They've got Solo, we've got The Lead Station. They've got Camden Market, we've got independents like Nood. They've got meedja types and musicians living there, we've got, well, people who hope one day to live in Camden. Basically Chorlton has got some great little bars making the trip into the centre of town often not worth the effort.

■ ■ ■ Polar Bar
Wilbraham Road (0161) 881 0901
Polar Bar is a trendies hangout and the place to be seen come the first ray of Manchester sunshine. The customers tend to get younger as the day goes on – beginning with the same four OAPs, moving to suits at lunchtime and finally the young Chorltonites after dark. The food in here is OK – making it one of the most popular places to eat in Chorlton. Light and spacious with plenty of seating, it's a good place for lazing away a Sunday afternoon, but be warned of the officious bar staff who wet themselves if you're still drinking gone 11pm.
Mon-Sat 11am-11pm, Sun 11am-10.30pm (food stops at 8.30pm)
Meal for two: £29 (Barramundi Steak)

■ ■ ■ The Purveyor
Wilbraham Road (0161) 881 0202
Deep squishy leather armchairs and calm ambience enjoyed by a sedate mix of young and old. I'm convinced that out the back they've got a cow tethered in a rustic yard, where a commune of people are busily making fresh cheeses and ice-creams from the milk produced by Daisy. They've all probably got names such as Sky and Jude, and all chip

in when it's bread-making day. The food here is expensive, but by God it's good and fresh and healthy (looking), and lets face it, keeping Daisy in organic feed isn't going to come cheap is it? Inside is totally non-smoking, in keeping with the holier than thou philosophy this places oozes.

Mon-Sun 10am-10pm
Meal for two: £24.80 (Linguini)

■ ■ ■ Lead Station

99 Beech Road (0161) 881 5559

This bar is a hive of activity day or night. The perfect place for meeting friends, sampling the self-indulgent food menu or just reading the Sunday papers. The most gay-friendly bar in the area, you're guaranteed service with a smile. Still, make sure you've got your best trainers on and the right street casual gear, as the Lead Station is a favourite with the fashionable urbanites of South Manchester. Décor is impressive, with a living room feel and walls adorned with contemporary works from the bohemian locals. For a two-course taste sensation on a budget try the early bird menu, weekdays before 7pm.

Mon-Thu 11-11, Sat 10-11pm, Sun 10-10.30
Meal for two: £27.40 (Grilled Salmon Fillets)

■ ■ ■ Didsbury Village

For the young, good-looking, stylish and yet slightly townie, Didsbury is Mecca.

■ ■ ■ Parisa

Wilmslow Road (0161) 434 1011

The perfect place for a sunny days skiving. Ahhhhh, lovely. But all things change come the weekend. The calm tranquil ambience is replaced by manic service, and tables of bemused diners surrounded by increasing numbers of drinkers (and some pretty heavy smokers) shuffling and pushing up against your table. The general clientele of Parisa is very straight-laced, with the odd token scally who's saved up a month to take their date to enjoy what they consider to be really posh nosh. A major plus point is the 250 long list of wines, and the fact that they sell it like an off-licence, reducing the prices for take out so you can drink in more pleasant surroundings – like home.

Mon-Sat 8am-11pm, Sun 10.30-10.30pm
Meal for two: £27.50 (Thyme Duck)

■ ■ ■ Pitcher and Piano

School Lane (0161) 448 9326

It's a tough world advertising. Brand, demographics, focus groups and other tossy terms can be heard aplenty when the MD takes the creative team to Pitcher and Piano to unwind. It's the kind of place Edward Norton from Fight Club would want to blow up – it's the kind of place I wish someone would. Corporate and bland it may be, but if paint by numbers bars with less personality than John Major are your bag, then you'll fit in here like the upwardly mobile palm-topped smoothy that you are. Enjoy.

Mon-Sat 12-11pm, Sun 12-10.30
Meal for two: £24 (Salmon Fish fingers)

pubs

www.itchymanchester.co.uk

Boozers, boozers everywhere. If the chrome-plated cooler than thou atmosphere of some of the swanky bars in Manchester is wearing a bit thin, then where better to get back down to earth than in a proper drinking establishment. Throughout, we've included food times if they serve food, and opening hours if they buck the trend of 12-11 Mon-Sat, 12-10.30 Sunday.

■ ■ ■ Manchester Centre

■ ■ ■ Athenaeum
Spring Gardens (0161) 839 7504

One of those places where you can sense the good ol' days are a distant memory. The venue space itself is wicked – it used to house a bank and you can still see the markings throughout the building. Large pillars, an elevated DJ box and a central bar concoct a grandiose image but the sticky carpets and lack of any real atmosphere mean you will soon be looking elsewhere for your nocturnal thrills.

■ ■ ■ The Bierkeller
Piccadilly (0161) 236 1807

It's a cellar, and it sells beer. Cheap beer. To beer-guzzling men. The whole experience is not dissimilar to something you'd see on Eurotrash – we're talking crap music, cheery Frauleins and grown men acting like apes. Though not gargantuan breasts, gurning competitions and dodgy porn flicks. Don't be ridiculous. Nor Antoine De Caunes. And what are you thinking? Of course Jean Paul Gaultier doesn't go here. Just leave it will you?
Only Sat 8pm-1am

■■■ The Britons Protection
Great Bridgewater Street (0161) 236 5895

A warm, homely, brass table-topped, nans living room feel offers the perfect environment to sup up one of over 150 whiskeys on offer in here. The Protection is very traditional, steeped in history and weighed down by character… no wonder it's hugely popular. A proper pub, that makes a really nice, snug change from all the café bars in the area. The Britons Protection can be dated accurately from its wallpaper – all the way back to the early 1800s in fact – now that's one very old pub. A special kind of place that you really should have in your list of top five midweek drinkeries.

Food served 11-3pm daily

■■■ The Circus Tavern
86 Portland Street (0161) 236 5818

The smallest pub in Manchester – and it really is titchy. In honour of this, so's the review.

Mon-Sat 12-11pm, Sun 12-3pm

■■■ Down Under
Peter Street (0161) 834 8778

Australian theme bars and clubs may normally be a bit naff – but this one's really pretty cool. More Coyote Cool than Coyote Ugly. It's a bit out of the way (not unlike Oz so far then), and situated underground (oh, maybe

that's where the name comes from…), so it can be difficult to find. The music appeals to the more discerning customer, with a real mix of old and new. The setting is very small and intimate, but the service is friendly and efficient and there's a cool chill out area out back. There's not a lot of room here – so if you don't like it, rack off.

Mon-Sat 5pm-2am, closed Sundays

■■■ Dukes 92
Castle Street, Castlefield (0161) 839 8646

Dukes is a must. Unless, that is, you're in a rush – coz oh my God the staff certainly aren't. Employ 'em young, pay 'em nowt, wait for them to move on and then we're back to square one with 'the great untrained'. The service in here is so staggeringly slow it's almost funny (but not quite). Ignoring that though, this is one of the best places to sit in the summer – with oodles of canal side seating, trees and peaceful pedestrianised surroundings. Inside the décor is classy – with antique furniture and huge sociable tables. Weekend nights it's rammed – which, dare I say it, makes the service even worse. Shame.

Normal pub hours except Fri/Sat till 12am
Food Mon-Thu 12-3pm, 5-8.30pm, Fri-Sun 12-6pm

■ ■ ■ Fringe
8 Swan Street (0161) 835 3815

Sat in the beer garden behind Fringe the other day, I wobbled slightly on my plastic chair craning to see the rainbow that the others were gasping about. My eyes remained skyward as I turned back towards the bar and I spotted the severed head hanging from the hand-made wicker tree, then I spotted the strange cross-legged man carved from wood staring back at me from above the door. As is so often the case, the rainbow indicated that the pleasant afternoon was to be replaced by a monsoon – so my drinking partner and I dashed inside where I sat on the rickety wooden stool situated directly beneath a rat pinned to the wall by its tail. My first, and last pint. Fringe – you'll either love it or be scared out of your wits.
Food served until 7pm

■ ■ ■ Grand Central/The Subway
Oxford Road (0161) 236 0890

Two pubs in one, this is the perfect place to sit and wait for 42nd Street or The Venue to open. With daily offers such as 'buy a pint get a whisky free' or 50p tequila, you can get well on your way to oblivion without damaging your finances. Grand Central upstairs has a pool table and Subway downstairs a brilliant

Indie jukebox – what more could you ask for? Just don't expect high standards or a strict door policy and you'll be laughing.

■ ■ ■ Jabez Clegg
2 Portsmouth Street (0161) 272 8612

This is a huge student hangout. The moral of that story being – don't bother going here unless you actually are a student. Set out like a playground for freshers – with cheap, canteen-style food, lots of machines with flashing lights, other miscellaneous pub games and a huge screen showing the football (with church pew style seating facing it). Jabez Clegg could probably fit half the job-dodging population of Manchester within its vast walls, and regularly tries with events such as The Bop on the weekends, and live bands on a Wednesday.
Mon-Sat 11-2am, Sun 11-11. Food all day.

■ ■ ■ Jacksons Wharf
Blantyne Street, Castlefield
(0161) 819 5317

Judging by the volume of officey types here on any given day, this is the place for working lunches, though God knows why 'cos the food really ain't that great. You can have burgers, wraps, curry, fish or noodles, and it sounds pretty adventurous, but they don't do any of them particularly well. And it's pretty pricey for fancy pub grub. But if it's sunny, and you're in Castlefield, Jacksons is a very popular place to be, which means service is slow and there's nowhere to sit. Crap then.
Food Mon-Sat 12-3, 6-9, Sun 12-8

■ ■ ■ Lapinta
Waterfront Quay, Salford Quays
(0161) 848 9000

A cosy little pub with very friendly staff (AKA the crew) all aboard a boat. Those of us who suffer from sea-sickness shouldn't worry though, because this vessel's goin' nowhere. Simple food offered up daily. Not likely to become a regular haunt due to it's location, but definitely one to seek out on a sunny Sunday afternoon.
Food served all day.

■ ■ ■ Lass O' Gowrie
36 Charles Street (0161) 273 6932

A haven for the local media community, being situated across from the BBC and often overlooked by the 'cheesier' students. A traditional vibe is on offer with an excellent selection of beers, wines, spirits and the food is reasonably priced and tastes…well it

Neil, 25, Illustrator

Where do you drink the bar dry?
Dry
Spooky. And go clubbing?
Sankeys
Big names, big nights, and for big food?
McDonald's
Big Mac. Where do you regularly buy your clothes?
Corn Exchange
It closed years ago! What can Manchester brag about, and what should it be ashamed of? Loads of bars, but loads of pollution

tastes like decent pub grub. There are plenty of alcoves and quiet corners to discuss your business, or the issues of the day, and the staff are friendly and courteous. It would also be pretty rude not to mention the micro-brewery situated in the cellar – you can witness the fermenting for yourself via the glass canopy in the bar (far more exciting than the rugby they show on the TVs).
Food served 12-6 daily

! 🗋 🔗 From	Subject
✉ itchycity.co.uk	Meal offers by e-mail

■ ■ ■ Mark Addy
Stanley Street (0161) 832 4080

Inside the heart of The Mark Addy, you feel like you're caught on the set of a 70s murder mystery, but if you do happen to see Agatha Christie wandering in down the sweeping staircase with its brass handrails and smoked glass back-drop – don't be fooled, it's probably just an example of the slightly more mature clientele that this place tends to attract. Outside in the rather fine beer garden, there's alcoves to sit in, seats by the river and lots of leafy stuff. It's all a little bit cheesy to be honest (and always smells of polish rather than stale ciggies and flat beer – quite unnerving), but it's in a great location for a spot of daytime drinking.
Soup and cheese and pate platters only – served all day

■ ■ ■ Moon Under The Water
68-74 Deansgate (0161) 834 5882

Wetherspoon's Mancunian flagship is based in the centre of Deansgate. Renowned for their lack of tact, music and atmosphere – the MUTW is worth a visit if the prices of other local establishments leave you with a headache and a dwindling bank statement. Two meals for a fiver involve the usual suspects in decent pub scran. The booze prices are criminally cheap and could lead to a dependency with a host of offers, ale for about £1-£1.50 and a pint of Stella for under £2 (a rarity these days). It's always worth having a look at the impressive size and structure of the building (it's one of the biggest public houses in Europe), especially to the rear with loads of room and an elevator option for the extensive 1st floor bar seating.
Food Mon-Sat 12-10, Sun 12-9.30

■ ■ ■ Mr Thomas' Chop House
52 Cross Street (0161) 832 2245

Situated about as centrally as you can get, this ornate, traditional, tardis of a pub is well worth a visit. Daytime it's suits a go-go, and in the evening the clientele also tends to be a little on the conservative and older side… but that totally fits in with the surroundings – the kids just wouldn't appreciate the antique furniture, original tiling and wide selection of vintage spirits and wines.
Mon-Sat 11-11pm. Food served 11-3pm daily.

■■■ RA!N Bar

80 Great Bridgewater Street
(0161) 235 6500

Downstairs looks a bit like a stately home with its bookcases, old paintings, polished wooden floors and leather sofas. Venture upstairs and the feel is more contemporary with steel girders, exposed brickwork and modern art dotted around the place. The food mixes traditional dishes with more adventurous treats. Booze-lovers are placated with the huge range of JW Lees award winning cask ales and seasonal beers. Even your dad would like it here, although I'm not sure RA!N Bar would want him, as they're self-consciously aiming for the young, hip crowd.
Mon-Thu 11-11, Fri-Sat 11-12, Sun 12-10.30pm. Food served daily all day

■■■ Sam's Chop House

Chapel Walks. Off Cross Street
(0161) 834 3210

Sam's Chop house is the brother to Thomas and has been here since 1872. Refurbed since then, but all in keeping with the old character. Lots of lunch trade as it's in the heart of the financial district. Houses an excellent restaurant which is busier than the bar on a week night, when the crowd tends

to be more mature than the average. As it's situated in the basement you feel totally cut off from the hustle and bustle of the city centre and trapped in a time-warp. There's also a seating area outside which catches the sun when there's sun to be caught.
Mon-Sat 11-11. Food 11-3, 5.30-9 daily

■■■ Temple of Convenience

Great Bridgewater Street (0161) 288 9834

As you tootle along Great Bridgewater Street, you'll see some black railings surrounding a staircase leading enticingly down into the pavement, and then a second one emerging just a couple of paces further down. From within the belly of this five-metre stretch of pavement you'll hear music. Now, you're bound to wonder what the score is here – but it really is as simple as it first seems – there's a pub down there, a very small pub, with a bar on wheels, able to fit no more than about twenty people. It's dead quirky, novel, yet very chilled out. But, if you can't squeeze in and you feel left out, then comfort yourself with one thing – those people are actually enjoying a drink in an old public toilet. Fact.
Mon-Sun 4-11

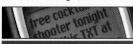

itchy sms @
www.itchymanchester.co.uk

▓ ■ ■ White Lion
43 Liverpool Road, Castlefield
(0161) 832 7373

You've taken the kids to the Museum of Science and Industry and they've screamed and whinged the whole way around about wanting an ice-cream, a drink, the toilet…they're tired, they're bored, and you really, really need a decent pint. An oasis is nearby – take the whole family to The White Lion. You can sit on the terrace outside whilst the kids play on the grass and climb over the ruins of the Roman fort, and everyone can eat some excellent pub grub at little cost. If you haven't had a nightmare day at the museum, it's still worth seeking out (after everyone else has taken their kids home, obviously) as there's a good wine list, plenty of choice on draft, and a friendly evening atmosphere.
Food Mon-Thu 12-8, Fri 12-6.30pm, Sat-Sun 12-5pm

▓ ■ ■ Fallowfield

Fallowfield is home to thousands upon thousands of students. Basically a ready-made pub crawl and if you're not a student, there's little here for you. Begone to West Didsbury. For the remainder, students unite – this is your cheap drink and kebab paradise.

▓ ■ ■ Bar XS
Wilmslow Road (0161) 257 2403

Formerly Fallowfield Police Station, Bar XS straddles the divide between pub and club in a unique way with its meshing of ear-splitting music, late licence and dolled up mix of clientele, with wooden, minimalist décor and inescapably pub-like atmosphere. A great move for those wanting a few more drinks after more appealing surrounding bars lock their doors, but easily topped for the rest who need a bit more character in their choice of watering hole. Small size and sticky-floor syndrome are other downsides, not to mention the ever-present trollied

PLAN YOUR RESIGNATION TACTICALLY

essential drinking info @
www.itchymanchester.co.uk

ball machines and tasteful yellow décor ensure the atmosphere is never solemn, (although it depresses me) while cheap and cheerful drinks make the clientele equally cheap and cheerful. Separate downstairs bar and upstairs cheese-o-rama club also partition the drinkers from the dancers, a true blessing for those of use who'd rather puke into our pound-a-pints than watch another student mating ritual.

■■■ Queen of Hearts
256 Wilmslow Road

Queen of Tarts (as its affectionately and aptly called) is the mother of all student nightspots. Spacious and buzzing with young revellers searching for a mate or on the lash with mates, this place is like a church of the alcoholics at the point where they've got one arm draped round your shoulders, a grin cracking their wrinkled features, telling you how you really are their best mate in the world. Queues inevitably form quickly on a Friday night, while an ample beer garden also serves as a magnet for daytime summer drinkers from all walks of life.

bloke on his own, always jealously guarding a convenient space by the wall. Has a Thai restaurant actually within the pub too – novel or what?

Mon-Thu 12-12, Fri-Sat 12-2am, Sun 12-10.30pm. Food all day daily.

■■■ Robinski's
Wilbraham Road (0161) 248 1931

Robinski's is part of the 'It's A Scream' chain and as such looks like every other bar in this clone race of student pubs, catering for the daytime lecture-skiver and nightime reveller in equal measures. The ever-audible jukebox and presence of giant Jenga, Connect 4, pin-

REMEMBER, LEAVE ON A POSITIVE NOTE.

■ ■ ■ Scruffy Murphy's
256 Wilmslow Road (0161) 256 0012

Officially the Tiniest Irish Pub in the World…Ever! Scruffs is the epicentre of old men masquerading as young, and young masquerading as old. As with all good Irish bars, the emphasis is on the craic, and to that end they have some quality stand-up nights, traditional Irish bands and a venue where you're just as likely to leave with someone you've never met as those you came in with. A typically wooden interior is adorned with routine "Guinness is Good for You" signs, leaving little to set Scruffy's apart from any other pub of its ilk. Small size serves to irritate on a weekend night as you jostle to the bar, but also generates a warm and welcome atmosphere the rest of the time, leading many to proudly call this place their beloved local.
Open all day when the students are around, 6pm-11pm daily in the summer

■ ■ ■ Glass
Wilmslow Road (0161) 257 0770

Glass is so called due to a transparent front-half, ensuring a try-before-you-buy policy on behalf of potential customers. A somewhat more exclusive joint than those of its environs, this place attracts a drinker with a fatter wallet and cooler music collection than most. Downstairs feels more like a café bar, while a trip upstairs, although slightly more dingy, does provide a balcony for those summer evening pints. Black marks include filling up very quickly when you least want it to and tin foil seats on the balcony. That said, Glass is a welcome break from the Fallowfield student layabout norm.
Mon-Thu 12-11.30, Fri-Sat 12-12, Sun 12-10.30. Limited menu always available.

■ ■ ■ Didsbury Village & West Didsbury

■ ■ ■ The Didsbury
Wilmslow Road (0161) 445 5389

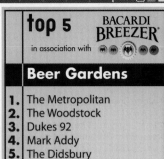

top 5 BACARDI BREEZER

in association with

Beer Gardens

1. The Metropolitan
2. The Woodstock
3. Dukes 92
4. Mark Addy
5. The Didsbury

If you want a touch of sophistication injected into your pub crawls – look no further than the Didsbury. Though it's pretty useless as part of a pub crawl as you'll never want to leave. Huge sociable wooden tables are mixed with candlelit tables for two, dotted in between banisters and beams, snugs and alcoves – there's also a large no smoking area (what a waste). In the summer, the Fletcher Moss Park is just behind and there's a beer garden out front, and in the winter there's three fires and plenty of chatter over red wine. The food at The Didsbury is splendid – from pub type snacks to the full-on restaurant menu. We can't recommend this pub enough. There's always a down-side though, and here it would have to be that it can get a bit too busy... but there's a very good reason for that.
Food served all day.

■ ■ ■ The Dog & Partridge
667 Wilmslow Road (0161) 445 5322

A proper spit 'n' sawdust sort of pub – but maybe 'flat beer 'n' peanut shells' is more accurate. Rustic, simple, friendly and very hot when busy. On the posing parade that is Didsbury Village, it's a welcome retreat, a first choice drinking hole every time – every time that is except for on a Wednesday, when it's quiz night. I won't say anymore.

■ ■ ■ The Railway
Lapwing Lane, West Didsbury

It's amazing what a makeover can produce. Once a backward hellwater full of drunken old men, this is now a very cool modern drinkery. A bit like a mini-version of The Metropolitan over the road, but much warmer, friendlier, and cheaper – you can get a pint for £1.13. It's attracting a nice mix of students, locals and upwardly mobile suits who've emigrated from the aforementioned Met.

BEWARE OF THE VOICES. FOR CAREER ADVICE WORTH LISTENING TO, INCLUDING HELP WITH INTERVIEWS, VISIT 🔴 monster.co.uk

■ ■ ■ The Metropolitan
Burton Road / Lapwing Lane
(0161) 374 9559

Large, busy, and lushly furnished, this is another example of the face-lift that West Didsbury is experiencing at the moment. The Metropolitan is a classy joint with a bit of a buzz about it. The restaurant serves some really great food and does an unusually tasty Sunday roast (although their potatoes could do with some TLC). As it's my local I'd like to put in a special word of thanks for the genius that decided on the extension of the beer garden at the back – including outside stable bar. Always very busy indeed, and quite rightly so.

Food served all day daily.

famous or sat behind a big desk, and this lot are clearly neither. Coupled with a 'lights up, music off, make your way home NOW!' attitude that starts some time before 11, and endlessly disappointing food, this is an excellent prospect ruined.

Food served 12-7.30pm daily.

■ ■ ■ Chorlton

■ ■ ■ The Horse and Jockey
Chorlton Green (0161) 860 7794

The Horse and Jockey is where Chorlton's socialites retreat on a Sunday night, safe in the knowledge that Ken's legendary Pop Quiz will ease them into another week at work. Chorlton Green hides at the end of Beech Road in the leafy end of town, and from May to September is the communal sun lounger of its residents. While away a sunny day outside this place and you'll be hooked on the atmosphere – dark, cosy and, er, smoky inside, 'The Jockey' is your favourite local already. The only difference is most of the contestants on karaoke night have already won the Mercury Music prize…

■ ■ ■ The Woodstock
Barlow Moor Road (0161) 448 7951

Bunch of arse. Why? Well, it's looks alright – beautiful places to sit on a sunny afternoon, high-vaulted ceilings, comfy armchairs, art on the walls. But there are two big problems with this place. First off, the staff – now, quite frankly, if you're going to be arrogant, unfriendly and slow, you either need to be

■ ■ ■ The Famous Trevor Arms
Beech Road

Another cosy local round the corner from The Horse and Jockey, The Trevor is a friendly pub famous (to us) for it's good value beer and traditional darts board. Although fairly dingy inside, this definitely adds to the 'old man' charm and is the place to get away from the student population of Chorlton. Although The Trevor really isn't the place to boogie on a Saturday night it's the perfect option for a friendly 'swift half'. Or a lager top, or an egg nog, whatever takes your fancy.

■ ■ ■ The Royal Oak
Barlow Moor Road

Good for the football although probably better if you're a blue! The Royal Oak is probably the biggest pub in Chorlton and one of the few left where you can have a game of pool.

There's a function room upstairs, more recently used for the odd club night and the monthly comedy stand up show.

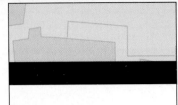

clubs

www.itchymanchester.co.uk

Don't believe a thing any moaning Manchester resident tells you about the lack of any decent clubs since the demise of the Hacienda. For diversity of venues and sounds - everyone knows Manc's better than anywhere else outside of London.

■ ■ ■ 5th Avenue
121 Princess Street (0161) 236 2754

A student-filled frenzy of 50p shots, music you didn't think you liked (until you sampled the 50p vodka) and people you swore you'd never fancy (until you tried the 50p whisky). The place smells of vomit, a smell that remains even after the regular foam parties should have washed it away. When you're on the too-crowded dance-floor, being felt up by some 16 year old girl/boy in mum/dad's cologne, dancing to the Housemartins or Northside, try to remember through your vodka-fuelled haze that, by day, you are a respectable human being. Just don't puke on yourself and you're laughing.

■ ■ ■ 42nd Street
Bootle Street (0161) 831 7108

Much like 5th Avenue, but a shade classier and bigger. 42nd Street is where indie kids come to grow up. The club caters for the more discerning pop reveller, with a more sophisticated play-list. The Beastie Boys, Stevie Wonder and UNKLE lie easily alongside the more standard Stone Roses, Verve and Charlatans. Full of those searching for Manchester's musical legacy and 25-year olds wishing it was still 1989 so they could go to the Hacienda instead. Most people out for a cheap shag generally choose 5th Avenue, despite the £1 a pint offers, leaving the 42nd Street crowd free to lap up the music.

Finger
tips

■ ■ ■ Ampersand
Deansgate Court, 244 Deansgate
(0161) 832 3038

Uproar in Manchester! Rumours have it that the long-haired lothario Peter Stringfellow is planning on turning Ampersand into a love-shack along the same lines as London. Which camp are you in? "Yes to lovely ladies", or "No to dirty scrubbers". Vote now!

■ ■ ■ The Attic
Above Thirsty Scholar off Oxford Road
(0161) 236 6071

Strangely reminiscent of a school drama studio (it's even got paper things hanging from the ceiling), the Attic's cosy (some may say claustrophobic) interior plays host to some of the best soul nights in the north. A friendly no-nonsense and no-trouble atmosphere makes for an easy-going night out where folks simply appreciate good music. Thursday to Saturday nights at the Attic are for one thing only – dancin'. Drunken stumblers should be aware of the rather hazardous spiral staircase and sunken dance-floor though, as the general view is that a night's less fun if it ends with a broken leg.

■ ■ ■ Berlin
11 Bloom Street (0161) 237 1611

Blimey, I've never seen the Village so busy, and it's only a Thursday, and it's heaving with straight people. That's because Thursday night is Berlin's most popular night, the legendary Kat Club, where the laydeez drink free before 11pm. Berlin plays host to birthday/end of exams/hen do's/any old excuse for a piss up kinda nights out. It caters for your gettin' down and dirty disco crowd, think Abba, think Wham, think school disco. The DJ keeps things rowdy with his bingo style shout outs, 'Yes! The lovely Nicola is 21 today. Big up!' Dress to pull and drink to throw up. You know the score.

Hot tip

clubsclubsclubsclubsclubsclubsclubsclubsclubsclubsclubs **clubs** ▢ ■ ■

open 'til 4am weekends
open late all week

berlin

11 Bloom Street Manchester
0161 237 1611
info@berlin.co.uk   www.berlin.co.uk

■ ■ ■ **Big Hands**
Oxford Road

Big Hands is one of those places for those 'in the know' – it doesn't seem to have any set opening hours, and stop going for a week and you'll find out some hot new superstar DJ has just played there. Officially the worst toilets in Manchester - take waders. The music policy is as varied as the somewhat freeky clientele, ranging from Northern Soul to local unsigned bands and the décor is just the right side of kitsch. It's tatty – especially outside, where it looks like it's been abandoned in anticipation of the arrival of the bull-dozers, but it's perfect for those after-gig moments when you really want more beer but you don't want to pay for a club.

■ ■ ■ **Club Underground**
UMIST Students Union (0161) 200 3286

In the heart of Manchester's UMIST establishment lies Club Underground. Into the student union building and guess what? Down some stairs to the undeniably underground – Club Underground. It's a huge rectangular shape with a solitary bar at the rear. It can be a pain getting a drink when it's busy because the one bar is diminutive. But that said, Sub Tub have enjoyed a good deal of excellent events here showcasing bootie shakin' hip hop/drum and bass. Other nights can be a bit sketchier, filled exclusively with students, but this is a student union after all, so they tend to play the usual job dodger soundtrack of indie, rock, techno and trance

RIZLA ⊹ **It's what you make of it.**

www.itchy**manchester**.co.uk   67 ▢

■ ■ ■ The Brickhouse
**Arch 66, Whitworth Street West
(0161) 236 4418**

You want an 80s night, or an evening dedicated to glam rock, or a 60's soul occasion, or a mammoth night of chart music and 90's classics? The Brickhouse has a night allocated for each, and they're all pretty decent. It's small, but the two floors help space punters out a little. The DJ is very hard to get to, making requests a tad tricky but the bouncers are ever so helpful when searching for a taxi at chucking out time, but they soon sort you out if there's any trouble brewing. Cheap, easy and pretty good fun. Near the defunct Hacienda, on the way to Deansgate Locks from Oxford Rd.

■ ■ ■ Club V
111 Deansgate (0161) 834 9975

Near to lots of smart townie type bars, and this club isn't trying to buck any Deansgate trend. Perhaps predictably for a vocal house and garage club, the punters are the glammed-up pouty kind, especially on their Saturday night, Venus. Don't turn up expecting to blag your way in here with ripped jeans and stinking trainers – you might chose to, but the bouncers won't wear it. Once you've run the entry gauntlet, it gets even more treacherous. Moody podium types in short skirts and knee-high boots, and Action Men with short hair and shiny shirts who'll get pissed off if you start trying to eye up their Cindy.

Flick through the papers

■ ■ ■ Copacabana
Dale Street (0161) 237 3441

Before you leave the house, dig out that sticky bottle of sangria you brought home from Spain last summer, put on J-Lo's CD and turn up the central heating. You're in for a night of dancing, tequila and pure fun. One of the only clubs where the men dance as well as the women, and if this throws you into coordination panic – well, you can deal with it one of two ways. The first is to go to the beginners salsa class earlier in the evening and then get up and shake your thang with the best of them. The second is to stock up on tequila and Bacardi Breezers,

get hammered and then when Santana's 'Maria Maria' comes on at the end, convince yourself that all those years of watching the final scene of Dirty Dancing has taught you some moves.

Basil, 30, Nurse & DJ

Where can you be found nursing a pint Basil? Baa Bar
And where do you brush up against the ladies on the dancefloor? Po Na Na
Boom boom. Where do you eat? Funny. Shimla Pinks
You seem happy with your clothes. Where are they from? Westworld and other NQ places
What's the very best thing about Manchester? The beautiful women
And what riles you about this city? Racism

■ ■ ■ Elemental
Oxford Road (0161) 236 7227

Next to The Music Box on Oxford Road. There's a modern bar on the ground floor serving some unusual sandwich combos and coffee during the day. It gets lively in the evenings with an up-for-it crowd warming up before going elsewhere or heading upstairs to the 1st floor bar space that leads through to a compact dance-floor and the third bottle bar. Tunes are generally commercial dance and pop from Monday-Thursday, with Friday and Saturday offering a little more emphasis on house and garage grooves. Ideal for a laugh with your mates.

Croxley House 14 Lloyd Street Manchester
t 07710 555512 www.emporia.org.uk

■■■ Emporia
Croxley House, 14 Lloyd Street
(0161) 708 8773

We haven't seen queues this strict since the war. No trainers. No slouching. No Burtons. No Top Shop. No centre-partings. And what the bloody hell are those white socks doing? With one of the strictest dress codes in Manchester, is it actually worth all the pre-clubbing preening, starching and ironing, stray-hair-removal, polishing of shoes and general ponciness? The answer's yes (apart from the shoe polishing thing, sod that, obviously). Vocal house and garage tunes are supplied by regulars who incl. Miss E, Jenny Harrison, Ben Burgess, Mike Antony and Lee Hussey. Oh, and for interested par-

ties – pulling potential 85% (unless you've got two heads, an all over body fungus or a rasher of raw bacon stuck to your forehead – but then you're probably going to Idols anyway). Entry £10. Every Sat 9pm-3.30am

■■■ Infinity
Peter Street (0161) 839 1112

"Me lovin' it, lovin' it, lovin' it, me lovin' it like that. C'mmon, everyone IS IT IS IT WICKED! Whooh yeah, we are havin' it tonight". I'm sure you are sir, I'm sure you are. You see, although Discotheque Royals may be dead and gone, Infinity fills the cheesy dance club gap it left behind. Their main attraction is their house and garage nights at the weekend, attracting special guests like MJ Cole,

Hand book

Spiller and Robbie Craig. These nights are over 20s only, with a 'make an effort' dress code (dig out that boob tube and leggings ladies). However, other nights such as School Disco are spine-chillingly aptly named.

■ ■ ■ Jilly's Rockworld
65 Oxford Road (0161) 236 9971
On the rock ladder, you start with Europe, work your way up to Def Leppard, followed by a dose of Sisters of Mercy, before diving head first into the moshy pit of Jilly's Rockworld. A paradise for old rockers and nu-

metallers, Jilly's is somewhat an institution in Manchester. Parts of the night will have you reminiscing ("I'd forgotten all about The Mission") and rocking with the best of them, others will be bringing you up to date with the latest Limp Bizkit and Eminem.

■ ■ ■ The Late Room
Peter Street (0161) 833 3000
The Late Room is a club that aims itself at an older, dare I say more sophisticated audience – basically it's your Mum's mates and brogue-shoed thirty-something's. The Late Room also plays host to a variety of acts from young upstarts to has-beens and never-dids. Deserves a slap on the wrist, however, for the terribly inappropriate music played between bands (nice bit of R Kelly, anyone?). Every night it's darkly lit and glossy, but the attempts at classy decor make it feel like a chain pub. It's a serviette-with-your-beer kind of venue – not exactly rock'n'roll and not popular with Manchester young'uns. Kind of place you're likely to accidentally pull your mates mum.

■ ■ ■ Matt & Phreds Jazz Club
Oldham Street (0161) 661 7494
When I think of Jazz (as well as a practically uncontrollable urge to say 'nice') I have a picture of candlelit tables, bottles of wine/whisky on the rocks, a sophisticated late twenties crowd wearing predominantly black and an up-tight pretentious atmosphere that is punctuated by the odd avant-garde poetry reading for good measure. When it comes to Matt & Phreds I'm right, right, right, right and then, totally wrong. Live music every night, and a very chilled atmosphere makes for a cool place to meet up early in the evening, but chances are you'll stay all night, cover the table in empty bottles and spend half an hour trying to find your way back from the loo.

RIZLA + It's what you make of it.

■ ■ ■ The Music Box
65 Oxford Road (0161) 236 9971

Located beneath Jilly's, this place is like a nuclear bunker. Hosting some of the most talked about nights in Manchester, such as Decadance and The Electric Chair, it's smoky and atmospheric, and great if all you want to do is dance. But by golly it gets hot in here – now I know some like it hot, but we're talkin' absolutely steaming. A second, smaller room is often used as the chill out zone, although again there's nowhere to sit. If you think that you might need the loo anytime in the next hour and a half – then set off for the queues immediately, because queue you will, be you woman or man. When you do get there, the cruel bright lighting and numerous mirrors lead to a scary parade of gurning partygoers wiping the sweat and dirt from their faces. The bar choice is limited with a few selected spirits, bottles of water and cans of Red Stripe. Not a place for sitting and chatting, you will be expected to be "mad-fer-it" at all times.

■ ■ ■ North
Oldham Street / Tib Street Junction
(0161) 839 1989

A really impressive up-for-it and friendly atmosphere is created by great music, people who've really made an effort and a venue that's perfect for the job. North is a club for dancing. The bar area greets you as you first walk in, but after that you're lured into layer upon layer of clubbers between you and a very hot, sweaty looking DJ stuck up in the far corner. Proper full-on whistles and glow-sticks type dancing. The girls are in some very skimpy clothing by the way boys, so that's always a bonus.

■ ■ ■ Paradise Factory
112-116 Princess Street (0161) 273 5422

See Gay section. Although one of the stalwarts of the gay village, Paradise, like so many places, wants to grab a piece of the straight action too. Trying to move away from it's exclusively gay image, Paradise is now much more straight friendly and with a mixture of forthcoming events devised to straddle the divide, expect to find something for everyone.

Take a leaf out of our book

■ ■ ■ The Phoenix
University Precinct, Oxford Road
(0161) 272 5921

The Phoenix is where many a fresh first year student has been initiated into the concept of dancing 'til dawn to a thumping techno soundtrack. Part of the 'It's A Scream' chain it's situated at the University Precinct on Oxford Road. There's a (sweaty) box shaped main room that can hold about 300-400 revellers and a chill out space upstairs in the bar for about another 200. It's home to the acclaimed Tangled night every Friday that has been packed to the rafters for over 7 years with a pumping mixture of techno / trance. Occasional garage, house, beats and breaks at other events costing about £5 across the board.

■ ■ ■ Piccadilly 21's
Piccadilly Gardens (0161) 236 7825

A classic of a night-club. In the same way that lumpy custard is a classic of any school dinner, or that Bananarama is a classic 80's band, or that… I won't go on. Basically, it's one of those places that has to exist because people just love their cheesy, townie nights out. Lots of leery lads wearing cheap after-shave, girls that look as though they haven't realised that Manchester and Ibiza have different weather patterns and the odd street scuffle when it comes around to chucking out and chucking up time. A local club for local people.

■ ■ ■ Planet K
Oldham Street (0161) 236 9497

Although it may appear to be primarily a house club, Planet K has benefited greatly from its diverse music policy, leaving other clubs out in the cold when it comes to selection. In any given week you might find the following on the listings: lo-fi live bands; 80s pop and trashy indie (at highly superior student night Loaded on Wednesdays); dirty dodgy drum'n'bass (monthly Fridays at

Spellbound); and electro, deep house and funk (Saturdays at Musik). The décor leaves a lot to be desired – basic pink walls and no mirrors in the toilets, although the lighting behind the bar is worth a look. A dose of Planet K should be taken at least once a week to ensure a healthy appetite for life.

■ ■ ■ Po Na Na
Charles Street, Off Oxford Road
(0161) 272 6044

I don't like the idea of chain-clubs. I get on my high-horse about the homogenisation of our city centres. But I eat my words when it comes to Po Na Na. Drapes, cushions, lanterns, booths and beds (yes, beds – great eh?), all combine to make this one of the sexiest, funkiest and most comfortable clubs in the city, and more importantly they've got air con, so you have to really exert yourself to get sweaty. The selection of nights includes a jam session with the resident band on a Thursday, and funk and soul nights on a weekend. It's this varied music policy and the intimate and friendly atmosphere that makes the Manchester version of the Po Na Na group the best one I've been to.

■ ■ ■ Prague V
Canal Street (0161) 236 9033

Nestled close to Berlin's in the Canal Street basin, this is an open, spacious two-tier layout. Inside there are seats and intimacy upstairs, bar and dance-floor downstairs. It offers a decent selection of beers and spirits with reasonable food to boot. Music policy ranges from commercial pop/dance to mid

prague v

P R A H A

SOOTHING BY DAY, HECTIC AT NIGHT

CZECH IT OUT

CANAL STREET MANCHESTER
0161 236 9033 INFO@PRAGUEV.CO.UK
WWW.PRAGUEV.CO.UK

week funk, soul and hip-hop costing about £3 to get in. Due to the popularity of The Kitty Club on Thursdays, Prague V now doubles up with Berlin's to provide an extended play area for all the cool cats and pouting pussies. The area is also very popular at the weekends with Prague V attracting a 'gay friendly' rather than a strictly gay crowd.

▨ ▩ ▩ The Ritz
Whitworth Street West (0161) 236 4355
The oldest club in Manchester and located down the road from the old Hacienda site, the Ritz is a world apart from the intentions of Fac 51, with possibly the most diverse selection of club nights in Manchester. They begin the week with Marilyn Manson fans crying in

corners at 'Dance Yr Docs off'; move on to 'Love Train' a 70s boogie wonderland; and end with regular grab a granny nights and Foam Parties. They also host live bands – Primal Scream, Doves and Rae & Christian recently stopped by. The venue itself is almost like an old cinema, with a bouncy dancefloor (honestly) and balconies you can spit/jump off (I wouldn't advise either though…)

▨ ▩ ▩ Rockinghams
Harter Street (0161) 236 5521
Principally, this is an old bloke's lounge bar affair but on Tuesdays it hosts a very trendy karaoke night (so we've been told) and Fridays and Saturdays see the continuation of the ever popular Harter Street Lounge.

For all those mourning the loss of Homoelectric, get your arse down to Rockinghams on a weekend to find the same DJs playing the same tunes to a scaled down crowd. It's just outside the Village, hidden down the rather sweaty looking Harter Street, but it's well worth the hunt. It plays top tunes, has some great tacky decoration (ornate guilded thrones, mirrors and drapes) and serves cheap doubles.

■ ■ ■ Sankey's Soap
Jersey Street, Ancotes (0161) 661 9085

This club has enjoyed legendary status in Manchester since it came to prominence in 1994. During its life span Sankey's has been credited with being a trailblazing clubbing venue at the forefront of urban regeneration. Based in the unfashionable and run-down Ancoats area of the city it's about a ten minute walk from Piccadilly into industrial decay yet attracts a cross section of clued up clubbers and party people that can be traced back to the original Bugged Out

residency. Nowadays Tribal Gathering has reopened the venue and it's the source of conflicting opinions, with many veteran 'Soapstas' yearning for yesteryear. Tribal Sessions is every Friday and features techno DJs like Dave Clarke, Laurent Garnier and Richie Hawtin. Saturdays is more glamorous with Golden offering elite house DJs like Seb Fontaine etc. Prices aren't cheap for weekend events and I know from experience the security can be a bit militant. Always worth investigating are the other midweek events 'cos you might uncover a gem of a hip hop or drum and bass jam where the atmosphere can be electric.

■ ■ ■ Satans Hollow
Princess Street (0161) 236 2019

Brothers Petrico continue the theme of sophisticated camp in their venues – where attention to detail and originality wins out over the corporate dronery of the competition. It's the Alton Towers approach to clubbing – pay your entrance fee and all your drinks and entertainment are free. Those who have experienced this genius before know to take it easy at the free bar – Satans is open 'til

Roll up

late so there's no need to rush to get your money's worth. The music policy is as diverse as you'll find – with a broad range of nights offered to suit all tastes. Get here early as there's often a queue around the block as revellers line up to enter Satans lair, and dance under the ever present gaze of the huge fibreglass figure of the over-lord. One night here and the devil's got you in his grip.

■ ■ ■ South
South King Street (0161) 831 7756

Tucked away underground on South King Street, South comes alive for Friday and Saturday nights in the city centre. For the past 5 years, regular DJs Phil and Jeff (a.k.a. Kane from Emmerdale) have pulled a crowd of movers, shakers and mod wannabes for The Rock and Roll Bar. The place to be seen for kicking off the weekend if 'Britpop to Iggy Pop, Hammond Soul to Northern classics' is your bag. The atmosphere is fun and friendly on both Friday and Saturday nights. The Dice Club runs on the Saturday, and if you're feeling lucky and you like to funk and D.I.S.C.O then chance your hand. The door and bar prices run on the roll of a dice.

■ ■ ■ Zumbar
14 Oxford Road (0161) 236 8438

Starting life as a room above a budget Mexican restaurant, the Zumbar club room has fought against people's elephant-like memories to assert it's position as a fine club in its own right. Small (200 capacity) and personal it offers a varied range of club-nights. Notably, Mini-Pop (held here month-ly) is the infamous and popular night that manages to attract some very sought after DJs, (i.e. Badly Drawn Boy) as well as many members of the Manchester in-crowd who love to bop around (oh so ironically) to the mixed cocktail of anything from Red Snapper to Britney and Madonna.

WORLDS FIRST PERMANENT
FREE BAR NIGHTCLUB

A FAB LEISURE VENUE

°NEO-DISCOTHEQUE

SATANS HOLLOW

INDIE
RETRO
DANCE
HARDHOUSE
CHEESE
TRANCE
POP

OPEN
MON, WED,
THURS
10pm til 3am

FRI & SAT
10pm til 4am

£10 - IN

DRINK AS MUCH AS YOU LIKE
ALL WEEK LONG

101 Princess St - Manchester - entrance On Silver St
t. 0161 236 0666 - www.satanshollow.com

THINK YOU'RE FUNNY? PUNK THEN WE NEED YOU

CONTACT WRITERS@ITCHYMEDIA.CO.UK

ances across the UK. This success results from the fine atmosphere created by a very popular blend of dance and house from great DJs. Keep an eye out for their appearances at itchymanchester.co.uk.

■■■ Electric Chair
Info call: (0161) 278 5650

Manchester biggest club night by a country mile, and rather excellent it is too. Electric Chair has attracted a fanatical following and sells out every month at Music Box. Tunes include house, soul, funk and hip hop from the Unabombers and some big name guests. Splendid.
£8, 10-4am, last Sat of the Month

■■■ Eyes Down!
Dry Bar (0161) 236 9840

Dropping odd numbers every Friday at Dry Bar on Oldham Street. This has fast become a mecca for those in search of quality beat music, with drum'n'bass, beats and breaks and the odd live drummer joining in with the action.
£3. 11-2am Fri

■■■ Friends & Family
Info call: Fat City (0161) 237 1181

Brought to us by the Grand Central/Fat City camp, this is the new incarnation of what was once Counter Culture, and by God it's good. They smarten up this scruffy venue and bring to it a mixture of hip-hop, funk, jazz and soul. Guests such as Richard Dorfmiester, The Nextmen and Qool DJ Marv... always well worth checking out.
Saturday @ The Roadhouse 10-2am

■■■ Club Nights

■■■ Afficionado
Fat Cat Cafe (0161) 839 9497, or call (0161) 273 3435

Afficionado is a free entry night welcoming those for whom Sundays are for more than just DIY and a quiet read of the paper. Jazz, funk, soul, house, soft rock, afro - the list's endless. Guest DJs have included Mr Scruff, Justin Robertson, The Chemical Brothers, Mark Rae, and Rob Bright.
Free entry, 6pm-12.30am, Sun

■■■ Bugged Out!
Info call: (0161) 950 3556

Originating in Sankeys many moons ago, Bugged Out! is now housed predominantly at Cream in Liverpool, but makes appear-

■ ■ ■ Keep It Unreal
Info call: (0161) 273 3435

There aren't many DJs who could fill a venue the size of Music Box to capacity on a monthly basis with a 6 hour set – but Mr Scruff does. Expect just about anything from one of these nights – jazz, d'n'b, reggae, funk, soul, house, etc.

£7, 10-4am, 1st Sat of the month

■ ■ ■ Musik
Planet K (0161) 236 9497

Yet another buzzin' leftfield night, with one of Manchester's most versatile DJs as resident. The Bugged Out! supremo Rob Bright is joined every Saturday at Planet K by a range of major league guests.

£5 b4 11pm, £8 after, 10pm-3am Sat

■ ■ ■ Paws for Thought
Fat Cat Cafe (0161) 839 8243

Eclectic to say the least – the resident is Brooks from Mantis recordings and you can catch DJs from the likes of Grand Central, Paper, Bugged Out!, Electric Chair, Fat City and of course Mantis (home to Atjazz).

Free. 10-2am, Thu @ Fat Cat Cafe

■ ■ ■ Sub Tub
Info call: (0161) 448 9431

Can be found at UMIST plus special appearances at clubs all over the city, Sub Tub can also be caught monthly at Cargo in London. More of a hip-hop/drum & bass night than any other in the city, it's for your skaters, snowboarders and student crew.

■ ■ ■ Tribal sessions
Sankeys Soap (0161) 236 9497

Very popular night held weekly at Sankeys, which has built up a fair database of regulars. You can catch the likes of Pete Tong, Dave Clarke, Frankie Knuckles and Justin Robertson…you get the picture.

£6-£9, 10-3am, Sat

Best nights for...

We know what a 'mare it is trying to decide where to spend your hard-earned on an all-nighter, so here's an 'at a glance' guide to what tunes are gonna be belting out from which club...

Drum & Bass – Sub Tub @ Underground (4th Sat of the month), Dry Bar (Eyes Down – Fri, Eardrum – Sat)

Garage – Emporia (Sat), Venus @ Club V (Sat), Satans Hollow (Thurs night), Infinity (Sat)

Roll in...Roll out

Hip Hop & Breaks – Sub Tub @ Underground (Sat monthly) & Planet K (Fri monthlys incl. Step Back, Spellbound, and Sub Tub), Paradise Factory (Thurs), and (depending on the guest DJs) Friends & Family @ The Roadhouse (Sat)

Indie – Pretty much every night at 5th Avenue, 42nd Street & The Brickhouse

Jazz – Matt & Phreds Jazz Bar – every night.

Metal/Alternative – 42nd Street, Satans Hollow , The Ritz, Last Train to Skaville @ The Roadhouse (ok, so I wasn't sure where to put this one – but it's a top night for all those into Punk stuff).

Pop – MiniPop @ Zumbar, Infinity, Magic Mondays @ Elemental (Mon)

Progressive/Hard House/Trance – Tangled @ The Phoenix (Fri), Synergy @ The Phoenix (Sat); and The Music Box is always a good bet on Fridays with Sunrise (techno trance – 1st Fri), Intergalactic Funk (3rd Fri) and Sci Tech (hard techno/trance – 4th Fri), The Red Light @ Sankeys Soap (dirty sleazy house), Foreplay @ North (1st Fri of the month)

Rock – Jillys Rock World, The Ritz

Soul & Funk – Funkademia @ The Attic (Sat), Po Na Na (Hiatus – Thurs, Slip & Slide – 1st Fri of the month), Northern Funk @ The Attic (Fri), and weekends at South

Techno & Electronica – Tribal Sessions @ Sankeys Soap (Fri), Havok (acid/hard techno – 2nd Fri of the month @ The Music Box)

Uplifting & Chart House – Crème Brule @ Paradise Factory (Sat), One Tree Island @ The Music Box (2nd Sat of the month), Back to Love @ North (2nd Fri of the month), Emporia (Sat), for a cheesy night try Hedonism @ Elemental (Sat)

World Music – Copocabana Latino Bar, Po Na Na (Wed), Zumbar (runs an eclectic mixture of nights)

OK, so now you can blag conversation with your mates, but if you really want to sound like a clubbing soothsayer, visit itchymanchester.co.uk. You'll find more information than a mere mortal could possibly digest, on all the monthly, weekly and one off events happening in Manchester's clubland.

At itchymanchester.co.uk, you'll find articles from some of the best independent mags . Here are just some of them...

 Big Daddy: Hip hop, beats and culture

 Juice: The UK Garage Bible

 Knowledge: Drum'n' bass and breakbeat

 Straight no Chaser: Jazz and all things funky

 Playlouder.com: Like NME but a lot better

 www.rizla.com

Factory Paradise

Friday & Saturday
*A strict majority lesbian and gay door policy
will be in operation*

Sunday to Thursday
Student nights including Release & Sensations

*Underground nights featuring Djs such as
Cash Money (USA), Marcus Intalex
& Deejay Punk Roc plus many more...*

Available for private hire

**112-116 Princess St. Manchester
tel : 0161 273 5422 (club) or 0161 228 2966 (promotions office**

gay

www.itchymanchester.co.uk

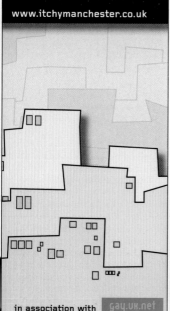

in association with gay.uk.net

The City of Manchester has a vibrant gay community, probably the largest and certainly the most visible outside London. We know its old hat chaps, but let us not forget the irrepressible and malformed Canal Street sign i.e. the first letters of both words have been removed. Manchester is, as we know, famous for Corrie, The Bee Gees, and Anthony Burgess. We, however, reckon it's more celebrated for having one of the most fantastic "villages" for the scene. Oh Betty, put that hotpot away darling, we're ready to rock, not rumble.

The Gay Village

Clubs

Cruz 101
Princess Street (0161) 237 1554
This is meant to be the safest gay clubbing experience in the city – and I guess in some ways it is. There's very little chance of any trouble in this place, which is probably due to the vigilant door staff and the fact that you have to be a member to get in (although membership is usually available on the door). Cruz has different offerings through the week – with a choice of drink

offers and varying types of music from disco to dance. There's two floors on Mondays and weekends with more hardcore dance on the lower floor and cheesy pop upstairs. It tends to be a good, hassle free night out any night of the week with a good chance of pulling, if you're out for that.

Essential
Minshall Street / Bloom Street Corner (0161) 236 0077

Essential has undergone many changes since opening and is still trying to find its feet. Previously, it's out-of-the-village location put people off, but it's now developing a loyal following. Natural really, as it has lots to offer. Operating on three floors with a mix of house and cheese, its a little like a cross between Cruz and the New Union. Open 'til a staggering 5am Fri/Sat, you'll most definitely have it large here, but as it's well-ventilated and well-staffed with plenty of bars, you should have no problem lasting until the wee hours of the morning.

Mutz Nutz
Princess Street (0161) 236 9266

It's a strange place where Grunge and Glam go hand in hand and somehow pull it off. Running the now well-known Poptastic on Thursdays and Saturdays with its slogan of "We're here, we're queer, we sell cheep beer", what more could any self-respecting student or financially challenged gay man or lesbian want? There are two rooms that offer either that apparent gay favourite of cheesy pop or indie to mosh your brains out to. It also has the added bonus of the indispensable 'Shag Tag' – and no, you don't have to be Sherlock Holmes to guess the general idea.

You get given a numbered tag on entry, and all you have to do is keep your eye out for the tag number of that certain someone that catches your eye and write them a cheeky note to get their attention. Great for those who are a bit shy (or young inexperienced freshers). It costs around £4 to get in with all drinks at £1 (plus mixers, of course).

Paradise Factory
Princess Street (0161) 273 5422

Slightly out the village, this is one of the older clubs, it's been kicking about for around 10 years. There's been some changes too - at first, the top floor was for lesbians only. Then they opened that up to all, then they got rid of the balconies on the second floor and now they have put one back again (ooooh, will ya just make up your mind?). It's now the place for the hardcore raver with its mix of hard house and techno. All attendants would appear to be the beautiful people with toned bodies and perfect faces and, of course, only the best labels in clubbing gear. It's totty heaven, but your chances of pulling aren't the best as most people go to dance. It has priority entry for those people going on to the Breakfast Club at Manto's but you'll still have to pay to get in. Also note that Paradise Factory is only gay at the weekends.

gaia

Lounge Bar & Restaurant
calm in the storm

46 Sackville Street t: 0161 228 1002

■■ Hollywood Show Bar
Bloom Street (0161) 236 6151
If you're gay and in Manchester for any length of time, you'll end up in here at some point, however hard you try to avoid it. It's camp to the extreme and a little grotty but tends to be full most nights and has a good atmosphere.

■■ Café Bars

■■ Gaia
46 Sackville Street (0161) 228 1002
Gaia apparently means Mother Earth. Hmm, if she saw all the leather used on the couches, she'd spin in her grave I'm sure. But this is one of those places where you can sit and contemplate your day, and feel suitably sophisticated in a soothing environment. It's the place to talk and chill – there's no loud music and the lighting is subtle and relax-

ing. Kind of like a classy restaurant or hotel lobby. They serve food as well but like the interior, it's not cheap. A great place all round to take your friends, sit with a bottle of wine or two and just chat.
Mon-Wed 12-12 , Thu 12-1am , Fri 12-2am & Sat, Sun 12-12.30am
Meal for two: £31.85 (Pan Fried Salmon)

■■ Manto
Canal Street (0161) 236 2667
In the summer it's packed wall-to-wall when the sun's shining and the street beckons, but at all other times the atmosphere is very chilled. There would appear to be no in-between at this place - there's either some gorgeous guy dancing on the bar at five in the morning after a night in PF and you can't move for totty. Or there's one lone guy sat by the window on a Tuesday night staring out at the passers by. Who knows. As a place, it really depends on the atmosphere and what you're after. Something for all weathers.
Mon-Thu 11am-12am , Fri-Sat 11am-1am , 2am-6am, Sun noon-10.30pm
Meal for two: £19.45 (Bangers & Mash)

Spirit

Canal Street (0161) 237 9725

A year ago it was a great looking and stylish place and almost always empty. A year down the line and it's still very new looking, but they've scrapped the members only door policy and the punters are creating a buzzing atmosphere. Excellent food and drink, stunning looking and lively as you like. Recommended.

Mon-Wed 12-12 , Thu-Sat 12-2am , Sun 12-10.30pm
Meal for two: £20.85 (Steak & Stilton Pie)

Vanilla

Richmond Street (0161) 288 2727

Vanilla is one of only a few lesbian bars and stays open 'til 2am every night. It's a lively and friendly bar that offers entertainment, and though it's lesbian-orientated, they welcome gay men too. Inside, it's arty and inviting, and what with its own football team and events throughout the year, it's popular and deservedly so. Can sometimes be a bit cliquey, but give it a chance and I'm sure you'll love it.

Velvet

Canal Street. (0161) 236 6523

From the fish tank in the stairs to the plush seats, the name of this place really does represent its quality. While Velvet also masquerades as a bar (it's an important fixture in the village and is fantastic for dancing), the food they serve really does stand up on its own. On the dessert front, the chocolate pudding (basically chocolate and cream wrapped in chocolate and smothered in cream) is absolute heaven. The basic house wines are delicious and you don't need to spend more for an enjoyable tipple. The light meals such as Velvet Melt and

manto
BAR CAFE GALLERY

...10 years young
and still going
strong!...

46 Canal St. t:0161 236 2667

soup and a sandwich would feed an army, so if you're after something really light opt for the mixed salad or bread with olive oil.

Mon-Thu 12-11 , Fri/Sat 12-2am , Sun 12-10.30pm. Meal for two: £24.85 (Moroccan Spiced Vegetables)

Via Fossa
Canal Street (0161) 236 6523

A world of reclaimed architecture and furniture covering four floors with balconies and pulpits. The cavernous Via Fossa is always busy and full of nooks and crannies to sit and have that intimate chat. It's a firm favourite in the village and that's not likely to change any time soon. It's relaxed enough to take your straight mates and they won't be too shocked or uncomfortable by what gay men get up to. But be prepared to wait a while when you get to the bar, as the staff are much happier talking amongst themselves than to bother with details like customers.

12-11pm Sun-Thurs, 12-2am Fri-Sat Meal for two: £23.85 (Via Fossa Platter)

Pubs

The New Union
Princess Street (0161) 228 1492

It's the local turned into Gay Glam with cabaret live acts and karaoke in the evening and a more relaxed atmosphere in the day. Has a universal appeal and is visited by all age groups. If you want to be out and proud it's the place to do it, but remember you're competing with the rest of the pub! It's always busy no matter what the weather. It's also, probably the first place you're likely to go when you've just come out and want to see the gay world.

top 5

in association with **BACARDI** ESTD CUBA 1862

Gay Venues

1. Prague 5
2. Essential
3. Spirit
4. Bar 38
5. Via Fossa

Hotels

Hollywood Int. Hotel
34 London Road (0161) 236 1010

The Hollywood International is just two minutes from the main line station, and the word grand doesn't do justice to this major gay hotel. With a 24-hr bar, 24-hr room service, and a television in all rooms, who needs to go out?

The Rembrant Hotel
Canal Street (0161) 236 2435

It's the village's older man's bar and the men in it are usually in their best togs. As such, it has a lot to offer, including rooms to rent (I say).

Others

Clone Zone (Shop)

It's a gay shoppers paradise where you'll find that little something you kept meaning to buy for the coffee table or video collection. Usual run of gay paraphernalia, from special clothing, underwear, videos and those elusive publications that they don't seem to stock at your local newsagents.

shopping

www.itchymanchester.co.uk

Manchester city centre rivals any city in the north for diversity of shops. In order for you to maximise your shopping time, we've divided the city into areas and given an overview of what can be found. New stores that we've been promised include Harvey Nicks, an extended Arndale Centre (oh, God, NO), and rumours of a Harrods (do they think we're made of money or what?). "Err, what d'ya mean my card's been refused? There must be some mistake…"

■ ■ The Arndale Centre

Even a bloody bomb wasn't a good enough reason to start all over again with this shopping monstrosity. I've also heard a malicious rumour that they're actually planning to expand. OK, so it looks crap, but if you get over the external horror and venture inside you'll find that, yes, it actually is pretty crap. However, it houses all that is great about high street chic – including three whole floors of **TopShop/Topman**. And there are your other disposable fashion friends, **River Island, Miss Selfridge, Etam, Stolen from Ivor** (well somebody must shop there). There are shoe shops galore, **Faith, Dolcis, Ravel**, but take my tip and head for the

Arndale Market end of things where you'll find high heeled lovelies for under £20 and loads of beauty places selling your favourite brand mascara for half the price. Don't go too deep into this area though, or you'll end up in the fresh meat section, or even worse, the fish quarter. Some people have been known to never return from the very depths of the indoor market experience... probably sold as part of a job lot from a bargain bin, or used as the stuffing for a beanbag. Christmas is a blast at The Arndale, with the **Warner Brothers Shop** and the Arndale grotto putting on a fine show – oh joy. They also provide services such as face-painting for cheeky little Mancunian kiddies - avoid.

▪ ▪ ▪ Deansgate

Pretty lame really by anyone's standards, Deansgate should be the shopping epicentre of Manchester, but it ain't. It is, however, home to the only department store worth visiting in Manchester (come on Harvey

Nicks and Harrods, we're ready for ya) **Kendals**. Housing limited collections from labels that have their own shops elsewhere in the city centre – but at least it's an all under one roof alternative – therefore

avoiding the Manchester monsoon. Word of warning though – all those tired old jokes about plastic women behind the make-up counters and those armed with perfume guns probably originated in this store – if you want to go clothes shopping here, there's a gauntlet to run. Further along Deansgate, there's a **Daisy & Tom** – insisting that little children do deserve to be dressed in designer labels, they simply have to have the latest fashions, at any cost - they didn't ask to be born now did they? For book-

worms, academics, travellers, people desperate to find that last awkward Christmas present, or for those that need additional copies of this fine print guide, there's a very big **Waterstone's** as well. The most comprehensive range of books imaginable – there's literally (gerrit?) thousands of titles here, if they haven't got it, it's probably out of print.

▪ ▪ ▪ King Street

Oh yes, this is more like it. A nice clean street, never crowded, lined with some old classics. A bit like a mini Bond Street. There's a few swanky jewellers, perfect for a spot of window shopping with your partner; you can't afford anything in there, but sigh, maybe

one day. Asymmetric fringes are available from **Vidal Sassoon**, still churning out the same standard of haircut that made them famous all those years ago. For the ladies, we have **Warehouse**, **Oasis**, **Kookai**, **Jigsaw**, **Morgan**, and venturing to Upper King Street, there's a 3-tiered **Diesel** masterpiece, followed by **DKNY** (yeah, right, like I can afford to even touch this stuff – and the security guard knows it), **Uth** (unisex shop for high fashion streetwear, and damn fine it is too), **Whistles** and **Calvin Klein**. Blokes can go all gooey over the shoes in **Aspecto**, the crisp business-like shirts in **Pink**, the smart but casual casuals in **Ted Baker**, and the profit defying goodies in new shop on the block **Surgery** (always having a sale, everything under £25 or thereabouts). Just beyond King Street is **Hope & Glory** and **Paul Smith** – offering a vast array of shirts -

uniform for work, Deansgate at night, or that dreaded family occassion.

▪ ▪ ▪ Market Street

It's a street, it hasn't got a market (unless you count an ice cream van and a £1 umbrella stall) and boy, does it get busy on a Saturday. In terms of shops you've got **HMV** (big, impressive, busy), **Littlewoods** (only worth visiting for the pick 'n' mix), **McDonald's** (come on fat boy), **New Look** (don't knock it 'till you've tried it), **Shellys** (you'll break your neck in those love), **Schuh** (now we're talking), **Levis** (getting better all the time), **Boots** (toiletry heaven, with its all new beauty salon and healthcare services) and various cheap 'n' cheerful shops that close and then open again a few doors down. There's really only the usual suspects, all totally overshadowed by the utterly horrific eyesore that is **The Arndale**. Market Street isn't the nicest shopping experience in the world. Take a deep breath, push your way though the herd, and prepare to enter market research hell. Don't stop or catch anybody's eye if they've got a clip-board or they'll try to flog you a catalogue.

▪ ▪ ▪ Northern Quarter

The Northern Quarter is a lifestyle, not an area, and if you want to truly fit in when hanging out in the café bars along Oldham Street – you have to shop here too. **Arc** has grown into the Northern Quarter's favourite funk boutique, always good for a browse even if you can't afford to buy the outfit of your dreams. They stock a good range of labels, think Stussy, Miss Sixty, Putsch and

Boxfresh, as well as a few pieces from original designers. No visit to the Northern Quarter is complete without a trip to **Westworld**. A megastore of affordable urban fashion bridges the gap between the style of Arc and the variety of Afflecks. Plenty of clothes in here for him and her, this cornerstone stocks a mixture of street labels and own brand basics so you're never stuck for choice. Try to resist the comforting smell of fried eggs and veggie sausage drifting from the **Pop Café** above, and come on down to the **Pop Boutique**, a celebration of all things kitsch and corduroy in the Northern Quarter. You'll find dresses, shoes and handbags your Auntie Shirley would've died for, next to new and used Levis and flares. Just one word of warning though – remember what looked great on Lulu then may not look good on you now…Next,

what's Manchester famous for the country over with teenage Goths and indie kids? **Afflecks Palace**. A rabbit warren of stalls selling anything from corsets to second hand teddys (bears that is). Afflecks has been here for eighteen years, but that's a lot

younger than many of the items of clothing for sale here, and significantly younger than most of the people that wore those items the first time around (and maybe died in them?). Cafes, hairdressers and piercing studios can all be found within the vast walls, as can many an unusual character, and the per-

manent pungent smell of good weed. The smaller, but nevertheless significant younger sister of Afflecks, **The Colleseum**, can be found a mere dreadlock length away, and houses similar bizarre and alternative gear for the anti-high street brigade…if you're into scouring second hand shops for original retro chic and other unusual items, then you'll find this lot have done the hard work for you.

■■■ The Triangle

All those who have spent the past few years travelling around Asia will be outraged to find that the grunge-teen hangout that was **The Corn Exchange** has been replaced by an altogether cleaner and fresher smelling concoction, **The Triangle**. Times they are a

changing, and they've brought with them a rather fine array of posh shops. You've got **Jigsaw** – full of floaty dressing up clothes, and it's very own café; **Ted Baker Women** – brightly coloured T-shirts and great basics; **Karen Millen** – sequin girly floaty embroidered stuff for very thin women with very fat bank balances; **Calvin Klein** – see through stuff that looks good only on Kate Moss; plus **Space NK, Mikey, Muji, Jerry's Home Store**, a nail salon, a smelly soap

■ ■ Out of Town

■ ■ Chorton

Although Chorlton has a wealth of café bars, in other areas it's a little lacking… not least of all for shops. Fortunately **Nood** has stepped into the breach and provided us

shop, and the ultimate pit-stop for ladies who lunch, **Zinc Bar and Grill**. For the boys you'll find **Gant** – preppy Amercian Tommy Hilfiger type clothes for the Chino's chap. For guys who feel a bit more rad man, you've got the surfer, skating look from **Quiksilver** and **O'Neill**. The Triangle also houses a florist, a couple of cafes and nik nak shops for those essential ethnic trinkets. Oh and the toilets have sparkly sinks with Molten Brown soap and moisturiser. A haven of peace and quiet – strangely, they seem to have a secret policy of 'never too many shoppers to spoil your retail therapy'. The Triangle is what little girls are made of.

Jane, 21, Retail Marketing Student

Jane, you look clearly posh. Where do you drink cocktails? Living Room
Aha, thought so. And for clubbing? I don't go in Manchester
Oh. Do you eat in Manchester? From time to time, at Casa Tapas
And I bet you know your high street from your designer gear, yeah? Indeed. I shop at the Trafford Centre and on King Street
What gives Manchester it's gloss? The atmosphere, definitely
And it's split ends? It needs more variety for clubbing

girls with somewhere to find belts, jewellery, jeans, tiny tops, t-shirts and all sorts of oh-so-desirable oddments. The clothing range is small but eclectic - you're bound to find something to suit your taste, style or wallet. With labels in the range including Religion Denim, Jiggy, Gash, as well as some exclusive

London based jewellery designers. The helpful staff will help you pick something out (there's always a bloke in here asking them for advice on presents for the other half – "well, she's roughly the same size as you, maybe not as tall…"). There's lots of reasons to go Nood. Further into the depths of Chorlton on **Beech Road**, there's a small selection of shops, perfect for buying last minute presents - including an art gallery, a balloons/joke shop and a lovely little shop selling nic nacs and jewellery.

■ ■ ■ The Trafford Centre

If Manchester gets the Harrods and Harvey Nicks it's been promised, then it's hard to see how the old TC will keep its head above water, but for now it's the ultimate out of town shopping retreat. Avoid

Saturdays if you can, when it resembles a scene from Dawn of the Dead, the one where the zombies overrun the shopping mall, but who needs Saturday shopping when the TC opens its retail doors until 9pm weekdays? But what's it got to offer that Manchester city centre hasn't? Urm, **Selfridges**, and a shed load of Manchester football players. Selfridges has fancy hi-fi equipment, inviting beds, catwalk fashions and a lovely little sushi bar, but is anyone buying this stuff apart from Posh and Becks? For the rest of us, we trundle on down to the high street names and the bargain outlets. **Music Zone** is worth a look (most new releases £9.99), and there's a massive **HMV** too (where I have actually spotted David Beckham buying hundreds of DVDs with Brooklyn in tow). **Mango** is an excellent women's clothing store brought to us from Barcelona (very long trousers, floaty girly items and very reasonable prices). **Books etc** has a vast array of just about everything from the world of print, and an excellent selection for kids (there's also an even bigger branch in The Printworks in the town centre). Try to spare the time to pop into **Zara**, which at first glance offers little, but if you look again there's plenty of classy items

at bargain prices (particularly good for jeans) and there's **H&M**. Oh happy days for men and women alike – the TC is probably worth visiting for H&M alone, although while you're there you might as well visit their massive cinema complex, the bowling ally, the pool hall, the arcade and the king of all eateries, the **Orient**. **The Gadget Shop** is perfect for the person who has everything, there are simply hundreds of snazzy little items in here to make modern life easier, more amusing or simply to impress your

mates. A packed branch of **Oasis** is great for girls who love to sparkle – it's all the pretty accessories and latest hipsters you could possibly wish for, and very much high-street prices – a staple part of any fashion conscious girl's wardrobe. And then, finally, to bottom off your outfit, try **soletrader**, where you can find eats for your feets. It's turned a generation of kids in urban clobber around to realising that shoe shopping's the way to go. Funky shoesorama – suits u sir! Diesel, Boss, FCUK…

■ ■ ■ West Didsbury

West Didsbury is one of the trendy places to live, and trendy people need to be kitted out without always having to make the trek into town. To service this need, some excellent little shops have sprung up along Burton Road, and now provide a reason to actually leave the centre of town. **Sterenko** is housed in an old bakers shop and still retains some of the original features. Complaints are that the mirrors are on a slant and always make me look fat (no, really, it is the mirror) and the changing rooms are slightly on the small side. But all this is compensated for by an excellent range of Coca-Cola, Diesel, Hooch, Cat and Bench labels. Great for guys and gals. Just a few doors further down **Hub** is where you'll find any cool essential accessory a girl could want. Quite simply the only place to purchase a birthday present that you might end up not being able to actually give away.

IT'S THE MD

Bags, purses, rings, little-T's, knickers, shoes and lots of bits and bobs for the designer urban coffee table. Slightly cramped, you run the risk of feeling like a bull in a china shop whilst trying to take all the goodies they have in. At the other end of the parade of shops you'll find **Thunder Egg** and **Big Air**. Thunder Egg specialises in magical little finds from India – lots of beaded things and pretty jewellery, and you'll also find labels such as Rude and Paul Frank.

▊▊▊ Directory:-

Afflecks Palace. 52 Church Street ....(0161) 834 2039
Arc. Burton Road, West Didsbury ....(0161) 831 7454
Aspecto. King Street & Bridge Street..(0161) 834 4875
Books Etc. Trafford Centre, The Printworks.
....(0161) 839 4223
Boots. Market Street ....(0161) 832 6333
Calvin Klein. King Street ....(0161) 839 7821
Daisy & Tom. Deansgate ....(0161) 835 5000
Diesel. 74 King Street ....(0161) 839 8868
DKNY. 78-80 King Street ....(0161) 819 1048
Dolcis. Arndale Centre, Trafford Centre, Market Street
....(0161) 832 4206
Etam. Arndale Centre ....(0161) 834 6915
Faith. 171 Arndale Centre ....(0161) 834 1350
Gadget Shop. Trafford Centre. 0800 783 8343
Gant. The Trafford Centre ....(0161) 819 3110
H&M. Trafford Centre ....(0161) 747 3801
HMV. Trafford Centre, Market Street....(0161) 834 9920
Hope & Glory. Bridge Street..................(0161) 834 8941
Hub. Burton Road, West Didsbury........(0161) 448 9438
Jerry's Home Store. The Triangle ....(0161) 832 2121
Jigsaw. The Triangle, 39-43 Market St (0161) 839 9057

Karen Millan. King Street, The Triangle (0161) 839 9485
Kendals. Deansgate..................................(0161) 832 3414
Kookai. King Street..................................(0161) 834 7023
Levis. Trafford Centre, Market Street ..(0161) 834 0876
Littlewoods. Market Street......................(0161) 832 5272
Mango. Trafford Centre ....(0161) 202 9887
Mikey. The Triangle ....(0161) 839 5461
Miss Selfridge. Trafford Ctre, Mkt St ....(0161) 834 3924
Morgan. Trafford Centre, 44 King St....(0161) 835 1330
Muji. Trafford Centre, The Triangle ......(0161) 839 1166
Music Zone. Trafford Centre ....(0161) 749 2422
New Look. Trafford Centre, Arndale Centre, Market St
....(0161) 831 7638
Nood. Barlow Moor Road, Chorlton ....(0161) 860 0461
Oasis. King St, Trafford Centre, Arndale Centre
....(0161) 839 8430

SHOW HIM YOU'RE NOT INTIMIDATED

O'Neill. The Triangle ....(0161) 833 3663

Pop Boutique. Oldham Street................(0161) 237 9688

Quiksilver. The Triangle ....(0161) 839 8855

Ravel. Trafford Centre, Arndale Centre (0161) 834 1389

River Island. Trafford Centre, Arndale Centre

....(0161) 747 8414

Schuh. Trafford Ctre, 44-46 Market St (0161) 834 6521

Selfridges. Trafford Centre ....(0161) 629 1234

Shellys. Trafford Ctre, Market St ....(0161) 834 0618

soletrader. Trafford Ctre ....(0161) 749 8514

Space NK. The Triangle ....(0161) 832 6220

Sterenko. Burton Road, W Didsbury....(0161) 448 0108

Stolen from Ivor. Arndale Centre ....(0161) 832 2671

Ted Baker. 52 King Street ....(0161) 833 2438

The Colleseum. 24 Church Street ....(0161) 707 3935

Thunder Egg. W Didsbury ....(0161) 434 4236

Top Shop. Trafford Centre, Market St ..(0161) 839 5788

Uth. King Street...(0161) 831 9981

Warehouse. Trafford Centre, King St....(0161) 833 9510

Warner Bros Shop. Arndale Centre ......(0161) 832 7773

Waterstones. St Annes Sq, Trafford Centre, Deansgate

....(0161) 837 3035

Westworld. 59 Church Street..................(0161) 839 5252

Whistles. King Street ....(0161) 839 5399

Zara. Trafford Centre ....(0161) 746 3700

■■■ Record Shops

If you didn't already know, you're either woefully disinterested in music or over 40 – but basically Manchester's *the* place to buy vinyl, second hand CDs or anything remotely rare or unusual. Unfortunately, there just isn't enough room in this book to include everywhere. So here's the main places in the city centre…

■■■ Beatin' Rhythm
42 Tib Street (0161) 834 7783

This place has soul...man. Lot's of it. Soul on vinyl, soul on CDs. Plenty of northern soul 45s as well. But it doesn't stop at soul. There's surf, 60s girl groups and a fantastic selection of US psyche/garage.

■■■ Clampdown Records
10 Newton St (0161) 236 7636

CDs and vinyl, with an emphasis on rock and indie covering the past 30 years. Some of the vinyl can be a little bit pricey as many of the releases are promo issues etc. For those of you with a bit of class then there are some very tasteful picture discs on the walls. Mmmm…love the 80s…

■■■ Decoy Records
30 Deansgate (0161) 832 0183

Shock horror. A record shop not on Oldham Street. Specialising in blues, world, jazz and country. Well worth a trip for the more discerning listener.

JUST KEEP SMILING AT HIM

top 5

in association with **BACARDI** ESTD CUBA 1862

Record Shops

1. Fat City
2. Polar Bear
3. Vinyl Exchange
4. Piccadilly Records
5. King Bee

■■■ Earwaves
9-11 Paton Street (0161) 236 4022

A retro mecca! This is great for soul, psych, folk, rock etc from the 60s and 70s. That's just the vinyl. The CDs cover this and a lot more from contemporary bands and artists. There's also a great selection for you northern soul freaks.

■■■ Eastern Bloc
Unit 5, Central Buildings, Oldham St (0161) 238 6432

House please and keep it coming. Euro, US, UK, Detroit techno, electro etc. Decks in store and plenty of flyers to inspire you for Saturday night

. ■■■ Fat City
20 Oldham Street (0161) 237 1181

Fuelling North Western vinyl junkie culture, Fat City records is well known for good reasons. A must for visiting DJs from all over the world, this place consistently boasts a selec-

tion that is worthy of its reputation. With a direct connection with the ever burgeoning Fat City and Grand Central record labels, these boys are involved in the industry on enough levels to make you feel confident about their knowledge. So don't let the extensive and up-to-date selections of hip hop, soul and funk fool you. Specialists they may be, but narrow mindedness ain't tolerated here; if you want a tune, these guys will either get it, or advise you on where you can find it. Go digging in the crates here and find out why the Manchester kids have got vinyl collections to die for.

■■■ HMV Records
Market Street (0161) 834 8550

Unless it's been released on your next door neighbour's indie label, then chances are whatever you're looking for you will find it here. Pretty much everything is covered, aside from the obscure bands. Obviously, it's high street, and so pretty mainstream, but there are a number of specialist sections covering a lot of ground from 50s to jazz or dance.

WHATEVER TURNS YOU ON

Piccadilly Records
53 Oldham Street (0161) 834 8789

A fantastic shop. Punk, dance, funk, indie, psyche, classic rock, electronic and a whole lot more. The store is closely connected to the Manchester music scene and always has the best local releases. Very helpful and friendly staff.

Polar Bear
123 Deansgate (0161) 834 1230

Here's the basics – selling new and second hand CDs at the lowest possible prices covering pretty much every genre you can think of. Here's the philosophy – to recreate the 'classic' record shop where you can buy whatever you want in an unpretentious atmosphere. If they do have leanings towards a genre then they'd admit to a great selection of jazz and blues but they don't want to boast. Polar Bear cares about you whatever your music taste and there's no worries here about what's cool....music is rocking in the free world. Truly revolutionary.

Vinyl Exchange
18 Oldham Street (0161) 228 1122

You need to take a look in here. Or rather, take a day off and get your mum to sort you out a packed lunch. Two floors packed with quality tune to inspire your spending. Covering every style imaginable – almost, with a very special vinyl section. House, techno, funk, experimental, American alternative...deep breath...indie, soul, jazz. Do I need to carry on? Well yes I do, because I've got another line to fill. There you go.

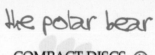

Virgin Megastore
Market Street (0161) 833 1111

How we love your shiny discs, so beautiful to behold and devastatingly dashing to the ear. The eclectic selection, elegantly racked throughout a carpeted paradise. The nymph-like speed with which the masters of music hunt out your heart's desire. And oh! The magnificent, splendorous prices – they make me quiver with desire.

Vox Pop Records
34 Oldham Street (0161) 237 5767

Second hand vinyl shops are alive and well in Manchester and this is another example. Lots here including soul and funk, good for northern soul too.

! 🗋 🖉 From	Subject
✉ itchycity.co.uk	Gig news via e-mail

entertainment

www.itchymanchester.co.uk

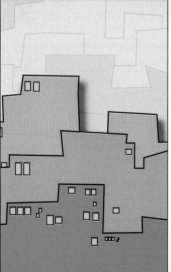

A selection of the finest entertainments that Manchester has to offer. Actually, there's some right duff stuff in here – check the reviews before you go eh?

Bowling

Megabowl
White City Retail Park (0161) 876 5084

Too often over-looked when thinking of possibilities for an evening out – bowling is the new black. Megabowl has all the facilities you could wish for, including a bar, which always makes the game more interesting (I also find that a couple of stiff drinks makes putting those shoes on a bit more bearable).
Mon-Fri 12pm-12am, Sat/Sun 10am-12am
Price per game – £3.50 Adult, £2.50 Children

Cinemas

Cine City
Wilmslow Rd, Withington (0161) 445 8181
It may not always have the choice of the multiplexes, but as one of the oldest cinemas in Britain, and still retaining some of its original features, it's got a lot of character. Friendly staff, dirty cheap tickets and a handy location, plus occasional 'classics' screenings and some of the smaller movies

the bigger picture houses don't bother to show, make it all in all a good cheap 'n' cheerful night out.

£2.75 students & concessions (ID required), £3.75 adults and all seats Sundays and bank holidays

UGC

Off Kingsway, Parrswood, Didsbury (0161) 434 0909

At last, no need to make the journey into town for your cinema fix. I'm not going to lie to you, this is not the swankiest, plushest or best laid out cinema I've ever visited - if you live in Didsbury then it's worth going to, but there are plenty of better cinemas.

£5.00 Adults, £2.95 Children, £3.25 Conc. Late screenings on Fri-Sat 11.45pm ish.

Odeon

Oxford Street (0161) 236 9778

Gives the impression of being Manchester's main city centre cinema. Inside you'll find the normal array of noisy kids, uncomfy seats and soggy nachos.

Late showings 11pm Fri-Sat
£4.70 Adults (£3.70 before 6pm), £3.70 Children

Cornerhouse

70 Oxford Street (0161) 200 1500

I have watched many an artsy foreign film in the minimalist surrounds of the Cornerhouse cinema. If you've ever wanted to go to the cinema on your own, but never had the guts, then the Cornerhouse is the place for you – you're not a Billy no-mates, you're frighteningly intelligent. And it's not just art-house films on offer here, oh no, you get workshops, lectures, question and answer sessions with bone-fide celebs and then some.

£5.75 Adults, £3.75 Children, £2.75 Students/concessions

The Filmworks – UCI

The Printworks (0161) 385 8000

It's about bleedin' time Manchester got to see how the other half lives. And by the other

half, I mean the Americans. The Filmworks is on a par with cinemas in New York's Times Square. If you're feeling really swanky, you can fork out £15 for a sofa-style seat in the Gallery, where you get free nibbles and waiter service. And the piece de résistance? The IMAX experience – wow, it's like you can just reach out and touch everything maaaaaan.

Late showings 11pm
£5.75 Adults, £3.75 Children, £2.75 Students

The Trafford Centre – UCI

The Dome 08700 102030

If you live out of town and want to drive to the cinema this is the place for you – you're always guaranteed a parking space.

Midnight showings for over 18s only
£5.65 Adults, £2.95 Children, £4.65 Students

■■■ Comedy Venues

■■■ The Buzz Club

The Southern, Chorlton (0161) 440 8662

Comedy in itself surely – cramming the masses into a tiny packed room in the attic above a vast, empty pub. That said, don't laugh too soon as the Buzz plays host to some of the finest comedians on the circuit. With the greatest respect, though, Mr Agra Man, who talks in crazy anagrams, you are not one of them, we ressot.

Thu 7-late

■■■ The Comedy Store

Deansgate Locks. 08705 932 932

The Comedy Store, like most of Deansgate Locks, is a little bit swish. Inside the club itself, it's theatre style seating, so it can feel a bit less relaxed than the other comedy venues. Having said that, you can drink and smoke in there – thank God. If you're either too drunk to care, brave, attention seeking or just plain daft then sit on the front row and you are guaranteed to become part of the act. Attracts some of the best in the business including characters like Perrier winner Rich Hall, local topical comedy team, 'Men At Work' and the World-Famous 'Comedy Store Players'. Clean, comfortable, and the only Comedy Store outside of London - posh or what?

Open at 8 everyday, late performances 1.30am Sat. Discounts for students and nurses Wed-Sat. Bar food also served.

■■■ The Frog & Bucket

102 Oldham Street (0161) 236 9805

A proper Northern comedy venue. The Frog and Bucket is basically a pub, but a pub with

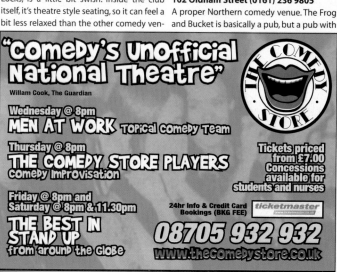

a stage and live comedy on it every night. You're much better getting a table on the upstairs balcony where you're at least guaranteed some leg room. Downstairs you'll really have to hold on until the break to queue for the toilets – coz you won't want to run (or rather climb) the gauntlet to the gents across the front of the stage. Friendly, and always busy, it's the most traditional and authentic city centre comedy venue.

Open 7.30-1am Mon-Thu, 7.30-2am Fri-Sat

Other venues with comedy nights include:-
Britons Protection
Contact Theatre
The Dancehouse Theatre
The Green Room
The Late Room
The Royal Exchange Theatre
See itchymanchester.co.uk for details

■ ■ ■ Galleries

With the rise of café-bar culture in Manchester, many up and coming young artists are now choosing to exhibit in bars and restaurants rather than the established galleries. In fact, you're more likely to be gazing at the next Damien Hirst in bars such as Centro, the Green Room and the Lead Station, and restaurants like Pizza Express in West Didsbury and Manto on Canal Street for examples (see relevant sections in this guide for details).

■ ■ ■ Blyth Gallery
Amazon House, Brazil St (0161) 236 1004
This small gallery is located within Blyth's Art Shop and is more an extension of the shop

than an actual gallery. However, they do have interesting works on display from international artists, as well as workshops the public can join in with, ceramics, sculpture and hand-painted glass for sale and a framing service.
Mon-Fri 10-5, Sat 11-3

■ ■ ■ Cornerhouse
70 Oxford St (0161) 200 1500
A 21st Century exhibition space – three floors of modern painting, video and installation – hell, they've even had virtual exhibitions here. People decked out in next season's urban streetwear, strutting around the gallery enthusing loudly about Tracey Emin's next project where she goes undercover as a cop pretending to be a whore who enjoys sex with dogs while chain smoking and filming it all to show to grannies who've been strapped to mutilated Ikea furniture or something like that.
Tue-Sat 11– 6, Sun 2–6

■ ■ ■ Chinese Arts Centre
39-43 Edge St (0161) 832 7271
Promoting Chinese arts and culture, you may think this gallery is for a limited audience. However, some of the recent exhibi-

tions here have been incredible, the only similarities between them being the nationality of the artist. The gallery space is wonderful, and you really do feel like you've stumbled on a hidden gem. With the exhibits ranging from sculpture through to installation via mixed media of all genres, it's well worth a visit.
Mon-Fri 10.30–4.30

■ ■ ■ Cube
Portland St (0161) 237 5525
Smaller than it appears from outside, Cube is a "centre for the understanding of the built environment". What this means, in layman's terms, is that there are exhibitions about bus stations and office blocks, alongside mixed media installations that wouldn't look or sound out of place on a New Order LP.
Tue-Fri 12.30–5.30, Sat-Sun 12–4

■ ■ ■ The Lowry
Pier 8, Salford Quays (0161) 234 1981
After a slap-dash opening when the paint wasn't dry and the lifts didn't work, The Lowry has now transformed itself into one of the North West's leading cultural venues. The exhibition space is marvellous with a perminent area dedicated to the work of Northern lad LS Lowry. The other galleries are used to good effect for touring exhibitions, although they have yet to prove themselves with a big coup. See Theatres section.
Mon-Wed 11-5pm, Thurs-Sun 10-8pm

■ ■ ■ Manchester Craft & Design Centre
17 Oak St, Northern Quarter
(0161) 832 4274

The Craft & Design Centre is a bit of a mishmash – a central area housing an open plan café and little else, is surrounded by 16 shops, display cabinets and suspended above it all is the strange (and yet oddly appealing) cardboard cow. Local designers, artists and sculptors, lease the units as workshops, selling the results from these small shops - it's always good to be able to chat to the artists themselves and see them at work. The cafe at the centre is excellent - see Cafe section.
Mon-Sat 10.30-5.30

gap between the Academy and the super-star-filled MEN Arena. With removable seats in the stalls to allow standing (and 'dancing' if Bjorn Again are in town…), there's also a seated area upstairs on the balcony, making it a perfect venue for both pop kids and thirty-somethings alike. Beware though - the sloping floors don't combine well with the plastic beakers of warm lager.
Doors open 7pm for performances.

■ ■ ■ The Whitworth Art Gallery
**University of Manchester, Oxford Rd
(0161) 275 7450**

The entrance to the gallery is bright, noisy and full of life, due to the gallery bistro adjacent. This is in sharp contrast to the first room you come to upon entering – for as long as I can remember, it has been dark, quiet and dedicated to textiles and prints. However, undeterred, push past this and you come to a spacious gallery lit almost entirely by natural light, which spans several hundred years of art history. The Whitworth's Historic Collection is internationally renowned, comprising of works by artists such as Durer, Constable, Rossetti and Ruskin. The Modern Collection is also wonderful, with artists such as Picasso, Auerbach, Blake, Gilbert & George and Hirst regularly exhibited.
Mon-Sat 10-5, Sun 2–5

■ ■ ■ Live Music Venues

■ ■ ■ The Apollo Theatre
**Stockport Road, Ardwick Green
(0161) 273 6921**

The Apollo has played host to many bands and comedians over the years, bridging that

■ ■ ■ The Academy/MDH/Hop & Grape
Oxford Road (0161) 275 2930

The University buildings offer a sliding scale for touring bands to measure their fame or anonymity. Almost every band has played here at some time or another, most starting in the small Hop & Grape. After your first album you can expect to be promoted to the larger MDH where you'll play in front of around 1000 people if you're lucky. However, once you reach the Academy you know you've made it. Reserved for stars such as Dido and Leftfield in recent months, the Academy will prepare you for the heights of venues such as the Apollo and the Arena. Just try not to get

MANCHESTER ACADEMY

Manchester University Students Union

Oxford Rd., Manchester. M13 9PR

THE BUSIEST VENUE IN THE COUNTRY
THESE ARE ARE SOME OF THE BANDS PAST &
PRESENT. FOR CURRENT LISTINGS GO TO
www.ticketline.co.uk / www.umu.man.ac.uk

ALFIE, ALL ABOUT EVE, ASH,
BADLY DRAWN BOY, BASEMENT
JAXX, BIOHAZARD, BLACK
GRAPE, BLINK-182, BLUETONES,
BUSH, CAST, CATATONIA, THE
CHARALATANS, THE CHAMELEONS,
COLDPLAY, DAVID GRAY, DAFT
PUNK, DEATH IN VEGAS, EMBRACE,
ELBOW, FASTER PUSSYCAT,
FEAR FACTORY, FEEDER, FENIX TX,
FLAMING LIPS, FRENZAL RHOMB,
GOMEZ, GONG, GORILLAZ, HAPPY
MONDAYS, HAWKWIND, HEFNER,
JAMES TAYLOR QUARTET, JOE
STRUMMER & THE MESCALEROS,
JIMMY BARNES, KATHRYN
WILLIAMS, L.A.GUNS, L.A.DOORS,
LAMB, LEFTFIELD, MERCURY REV,
MANSUN, MARCUS MILLER, MOBY,
MOTORHEAD, MURDER CITY DEVILS,
NAPALM DEATH, NEW FOUND GLORY,
NITIN SAWHNEY, NO F.X., OCEAN
COLOUR SCENE, PAUL WELLER,
THE PRODIGY, PUNK 'O' RAMA,
PURESSENCE, RACHEL STAMP,
RAE & CHRISTIAN, RONI SIZE, RYAN
ADAMS, SALIVA, SHACK, SHED 7,
THE SHIREHORSES, SNUFF, SOFT
CELL, SPINESHANK, SPIRITUALISED,
ST GERMAIN, STARSAILOR, STEREO
MCs, SUNS OF ARQA, SUPER FURRY
ANIMALS, TINDERSTICKS, TRAVIS,
UNDERWORLD, THE WATERBOYS

TICKETS AVAILABLE FROM:
Students Union Box Office : 0161 275 2930
Piccadilly Box Office : 0161 832 1111 (c/c)
Virgin Megastore, Market St, Manchester
Royal Court Liverpool : 0151 709 4321 (c/c)
www.ticketline.co.uk

too downhearted when by your next tour you're playing the MDH again – it happens to everyone at some point…

■ ■ ■ Band On The Wall
25 Swan Street (0161) 834 1786
25 years and going strong, Band On The Wall is like a vintage wine that just gets better and better. The only venue in Manchester that deserves its reputation as a true purveyor of global grooves. A typical week of events might comprise of salsa on Monday, unsigned bands on Tuesday, classically trained jazz musicians on Wednesday, dub reggae on Thudays, hip hop Fridays, African roots Saturdays and anything in between by Sunday. Go and experience a piece of living Mancunian folklore.

■ ■ ■ The Bridgewater Hall
Lower Mosley Street (0161) 907 9000
Home to The Halle Orchestra, but keen to be seen as more than just a bow-ties and boffins sort of venue – you can also catch more contemporary live music in this mag-

nificent venue. Not a bad place for a scenic cup of coffee either.

Check itchymanchester.co.uk for details.

■ ■ M.E.N. Arena
Great Ducie Street (0161) 950 5000

An American dream. Not only does the MEN Arena provide Manchester with a live music venue to rival London, but it also plays host to the local Ice Hockey (Storm) and Basketball (Giants) teams. Music wise, you can expect to see bands such as S Club 7, Westlife and Janet Jackson here – expect to pay around £20 per ticket minimum and abandon all hopes of actually being able to see more than stick men on stage unless you bought your ticket at 8am on the day of sale.

■ ■ The Roadhouse
Newton Street (0161) 237 9789

A veritable minefield of history, the Roadhouse is one of Manchester's great survivors (Boardwalk, Hacienda, International, where are you now?!). Currently the stomp-ing ground for every local band in Greater Manchester and beyond, it's also a key stop on any up and coming, NME loved, band's tour (such as Terris, My Vitriol and Breakbeat Era in the past two years or so). With sticky floors, torn drapes and broken lights, it's hardly the most glamorous of venues, but as the beer flows and the atmosphere hots up, history is made on a regular basis – Oasis, The Verve and Coldplay have all strutted their stuff on Manchester's best loved stage.

■ ■ Star and Garter
18-20 Fairfield Street (0161) 273 6726

A tiny ramshackle little pub on the edge of the City Centre, the Star and Garter could never be accused of not keeping it real. Most used these days for old punk acts, there are also regular tribute nights, such as Smiths night, Belle & Sebastian night and Manic Street Mania, a group of Manics fans who turned their obsessions into empire building. Look out in the listings for regular acoustic singer-songwriter nights too.

■ ■ ■ The Witchwood
Old Street, Ashton Under Lyne
(0161) 344 0321

It's official – this place rocks. It's been voted the number one 'PRS/Publican Music Pub Of The Year' and plays host to an abundance of local unsigned talent, tribute bands and big name acts. Prices vary according to the gig, usually only a couple of quid for unsigned bands, whilst the bigger names can command up to £10 of your hard earned. Based in Ashton-under-Lyne, it's a bit of a trek out of the main Manchester nightlife arteries, but by all accounts it's worth the effort if the likes of metal, indie or guitar pop are your bag, baby.
Mon-Wed 12-11, Thu 12-12, Fri-Sat 12-1am, Sun 12-12

Other venues with regularly live music include:-
Contact Theatre
Jabez Clegg
Life Café
Matt & Phreds
Night & Day
Planet K
The Late Room
The Lowry
See itchymanchester.co.uk for details

■ ■ Museums

■ ■ John Rylands Library
150 Deansgate (0161) 834 5343

The Gothic splendour and strict 'behave yourself' policy enforced by the staff will make you feel like you've wandered off Deansgate and into a time-warp. As you walk in the place smells like it's going to be boring enough to induce coma (you know, that mixture of dust and damp), but the stuff in here is so old (goes back five millennia – including the oldest bit of the Old Testament) and covers such a vast subject range (from ritualistic to medical), that it's really worth seeing.
Mon-Fri 10-5, Sat 10-12.45pm. Entry free.

■ ■ ■ Manchester Museum
University of Manchester, Oxford Road
(0161) 275 2634

Following extensive reconstruction, the Manchester Museum has re-opened its doors. It has very informative displays (if a little too stuffy – pardon the pun) on everything from the human body to the sperm whale hanging precariously above your head. There's also an area where you can see live boa constrictors, lizards and other slimy animals (How many times? They're not slimy – ed) – try and find out when feeding time is, you can see the snakes eat huge rats - it's an amazing sight. There is also a new Egyptology department which is cool (just don't watch 'The Mummy' the night before). The only downside is that they have taken away the working beehive.
Mon-Sat 10-5, Sun 11-4pm. Entry free.

■ ■ Museum of Science and Industry

Liverpool Rd, Castlefield (0161) 832 2244

The Museum of Science and Industry is full of fascinating insights into the industrial history of England. Great if planes, trains and automobiles are your bag, there are also good touring exhibitions, covering subjects such as Egyptology and dinosaurs, and don't miss the internal combustion engine for a really thrilling encounter.

Daily 10-5pm. Entry £6.50. Adults, children free apart from £2.50 for exhibitions.

■ ■ Museum of Transport

Boyle Street, Cheetham Hill (0161) 205 2122

There's no need to go out into the country to wander around the grounds of a stately home to experience the unique delights of a steam rally or car enthusiasts meeting. If you really want to punish yourself and a few of your closest friends, you can go to the Museum of Transport. In my opinion, there's

absolutely no excuse for wanting to spend your time looking at over 90 examples of vehicles through the ages, but for some reason people do, and here's where.

Wed/Sat/Sun 10-5. Entry £3 Adults, £1.75 Concessions.

■ ■ Peoples Pumphouse History Museum

Left Bank, Bridge Street (0161) 839 6061

Seemingly, the only thing we've got to fire us up for protest these days is this staggering collection of dusty old marching banners from throughout the ages. Though some of the exhibits in this museum are actually pretty interesting (not least the fantastic working jukebox). To be fair, the only thing that's likely to get you really going on an anti-establishment rant is a strong caffeine injection – have a fix from the rather excellent café bar on the ground floor.

Tue-Sun 11-4.30. Entry £1, Thu free.

■ ■ Other Atrractions

■ ■ Central Library

St Peters Square (0161) 234 1900

The Central Library is situated at the top of Oxford Road and dominates St Peters Square. It was only actually completed in 1934 and was the largest library in the country at that time. But enough already with that history stuff – basically it's a good landmark to know coz it's pretty unmissable, and it's a spiritual home for all academic and book-worm types. The basement is also

YOU'RE IN AN INTERVIEW

home to the Library Theatre Company (est. 1952), and see also review in theatre section. *Mon-Thu 10-8, Fri-Sat 10-5pm*

■ ■ Chorlton Water Park
Maitland Avenue (0161) 881 5639
You've never seen so many birds. And I'm not talking about the latest Chippendales show at Piccadilly 21's. Chorlton Water Park is a sanctuary for wildfowl of all shapes and sizes. Take along a loaf of bread, leave the dog behind, and the geese will love you. If you're the energetic type you can follow the walk along the River Mersey. It's a great place to go on a Sunday morning when you're hungover and moody (and no that wasn't the Chorlton Ness Monster in the middle of the lake – just Darren on a 6am post-club swim).

■ ■ Fletcher Moss Park
Millgate Lane, Didsbury (0161) 434 1877
Great for alfresco nookie, Fletcher Moss Park is also nice for more romantic or family based outings. In the summer, you can't go far wrong with a visit to the botanical gar-

dens (unless you suffer from hayfever), or a walk alongside the River Mersey, stopping at the bridge to have a quick game of Poohsticks. Later, grab a cuppa from the café before trotting down to the tennis courts to watch the sporty young things. Close to The Didsbury (the loveliest pub in South Manchester) for drinking when the sun goes down, and also near to the huge Tesco on Parrs Wood Road, a perfect place to purchase your post-pootle picnic.

■ ■ G-MEX
Windmill Street (0161) 834 2700
The building that was once the central railway station, the G-Mex is, quite frankly, huge. 10,000 square metres of un-pillared space, plays host to conferences and concerts on a grand scale.

■ ■ Manchester Town Hall
Albert Square (0161) 234 5000
You can have a tour around here if you're so

DON'T GET INTIMIDATED BY THEIR EYE CONTACT

Kim, 18, Student

Where can you be found having a quiet tipple with all your class-mates?
Usually down a pint or two in Glass
Of course. And where do you all go clubbing?
I love Music Box – especially Electric Chair.
You a veggie like most students?
Yeah, the best restaurant's got to be Greens
Nice clobber. Where do you grab a bargain? Deansgate/King Street
What drew you to study in Manchester? The galleries and culture
And what nearly put you off?
The crime and grime

79AD with turf and timber and then abandoned when the Romans left Britain in 411AD. The most noticeable sections have been reconstructed using sandstone rubble and cement which give the impression of how it would once have looked. A great place to sit and chill out away from the crowds (for thirsty little centurians, the White Lion pub is on the edge of the site and serves an excellent pint).

inclined. There's usually something going on, from jewellery exhibitions to Christmas tree celebrations. As a building, it's beautiful both inside and out, but dare we say – a little dull?
Mon-Fri 9-4.30

■ ■ ■ Roman Fort
Liverpool Road

Just off Deansgate, hidden only metres away from the bustle of the city centre lies a little piece of raw history. There are some original bits of this old garrison, which was built in

■ ■ Sports

■ ■ ■ Manchester City FC
Ticket enquiries – home (0161) 828 1201
Ticket enquiries – away (0161) 226 2224
Membership (0161) 226 2224
Merchandise (0161) 232 1111

Just for a change City got relegated last season, and lost their 254th manager since 1981. Kevin 'I'd luv it if we beat them, luv it' Keegan is in charge now. So expect plenty of

"OI, WHAT ARE YOU LOT STARING AT!?"

4-2 victories, ridiculous quotes by the boat load from Kev and promotion this season followed by inevitable relegation the year after. If you've not been yet then now's the time to visit Maine Road before they move to their new stadium in 2002. Who wouldn't want to visit Moss Side on a dark, cold Tuesday night?

■ ■ Manchester United FC
Ticket enquiries (0161) 8688020
Merchandise (0161) 8688567
Membership (0161) 8888837

If it wasn't easy enough for United in the Premiership they go and spend close on £50 million on two players just to keep things entertaining for the rest of the country. Some poor team is going to get a severe thrashing from the Red Devils this season, which should keep the prawn sandwich brigade happy for five minutes. And let it be said here and now that United fans are all

2-4-1 drinks @
Berlins before
9pm with this
TXT

thirst-quenching offers @

www.itchymanchester.co.uk

born and bred within the city limits - we irritated a few people last year by suggesting that half of Cornwall followed the team, and we all know that to be bollocks.

■ ■ Lancashire CCC
Old Trafford (0161) 282 4000

The other Old Trafford, Lancashire County Cricket Club also plays host to England's test matches. However, while the football club up the road goes from strength to strength despite the infamous Mancunian weather, the men in the white trousers are really not suited to these kinds of conditions. Take an umbrella and a good book, rain will almost definitely stop play.

■ ■ ■ The Commonwealth Games 2002

You may have thought it wasn't that big a deal. You may have thought the Olympics are where it's at. You may have imagined that Manchester didn't have the facilities or the money to accommodate 5,000 athletes and trainers from 72 countries. You may have thought all this, but over the past few months at least, you certainly couldn't have failed to notice that Manchester is the host city for The Commonwealth Games.

So what does all this actually mean for Manchester? With 17 events achieving a phenomenal global TV audience as well as thousands of visitors coming to witness the spectacle, The Commonwealth Games are

gonna be huge, as of course are the ensuing rows... is the council for the high jump for setting their sights too high? Are Mancunians polishing their javelins at the prospect of paying £251 million for the privilege? Do drugs really work? One thing's for sure – it's too late to pull out now.

Amidst all the festivities, the sports stuff only

actually lasts for ten days of fun. Events include; track and field, rugby, swimming, cycling, judo, wrestling, badminton, hockey, netball, boxing, mountain biking, squash, bowls, triathlon, weightlifting, shooting, walking and table tennis (great eh girls) Bit like ten mind-numbing Saturday TV sessions rolled into one). These events are spread across 16 venues – ranging from the breath-taking City of Manchester Stadium, to the Bolton Arena.

Surrounding the Games, there's a plethora of events planned from 11th March 2002 to 10th August 2002 by the Commonwealth Games North West Cultural Programme, funded by the Arts Council. Amongst the 550 projects planned you'll find music, dance, theatre and street performers. Further information on these events will be available in the special itchy Commonwealth Games supplement.

For those who's excitement button has still not been pressed – it's impossible to imagine that you won't at least fall in love with the charismatic mascot, Kit the Cat.

cultureshock
Commonwealth Games North West Cultural Programme

The Spirit of Friendship
festival
THE 2002 COMMONWEALTH GAMES

■ ■ ■ Theatres

■ ■ ■ The Contact Theatre
Oxford Road (0161) 274 0600

Lively, colourful and forward thinking, this charity-funded theatre hosts established artists, up and coming local talent, and groups of young people from local communities having a bash at small productions (some are infinitely better than others – but it's the taking part that counts). See itchymanchester.co.uk for up to date listings.

■ ■ ■ The Dancehouse Theatre
10 Oxford Street (0161) 237 9753

Sat under the careful gaze of the BBC building on Oxford Road, the Dancehouse Theatre is a hotbed of live music, performance and comedy. During the week there is everything from jazz to funk to guitar bands that are usually free although there may be a nominal charge for advertised events. They have started to put on comedy promoted by the revered Buzz Club that showcase leading lights from the world of comedy in combination with local talent. It also plays host to 'All That Jazz' at weekends, which costs about £5 and is a live jam of jazz and funk attracting a knowledgeable audience and a friendly atmosphere.

■ ■ ■ The Lowry
Pier 8 Salford Quays (0161) 876 2000

As well as the gallery of work by the man himself, The Lowry has two theatres, which play host to large-scale performances and smaller charity events or live music. One of the theatres has seats in it which were designed by Ferrari no less, and the biggest stage space outside of London. This larger theatre, The Lyric, has performances from well-known companies while the smaller theatre, The Quays, seats fewer people, but in all sorts of arrangements, as the seats can all be moved. Both the theatres enjoy the fact that the Lowry has plenty of free parking and offers restaurants, bars and cafes to visitors… 'a complete night out'.

■ ■ ■ The Opera House
Quay Street (0161) 834 1787

The Opera House, originally called the New Theatre, opened its doors on Boxing Day 1912. The theatre struggled to make any impact with a mixed bill and such diverse offerings as circus, tea dances and a full production of Ben Hur. Between 1912-1915, the building was bought, sold and renamed three times, finally achieving the name the Opera House in 1920. The theatre has housed first productions, direct from the West End, of Evita, Aspects of Love, Phantom of the Opera and most recently, Chicago. History lesson over.

■ ■ ■ The Palace Theatre
Oxford Street (0161) 288 6255

The Grand Old Lady of Oxford Street was born on January 9th 1889, and was originally billed as the Palace Theatre of Varieties. Marie Lloyd, Charlie Chaplin, Alicia Markova, John Geilgud and Judy Garland have all appeared here in smash hit shows such as Les Miserables. The Palace will make theatrical history again when the production of Miss Saigon premieres in November 2001.

■ ■ ■ The Royal Exchange
St Annes Square (0161) 833 9833

A theatre like no other – modern, vibrant and totally intriguing. From within the heart of the Royal Exchange you can't help but be in awe of this lovely space. Situated right in the middle of Manchester, the Royal Ex is a good place to get a coffee during the day, watch comedy, or see touring theatre companies. At least pop in and have a look.

■ ■ ■ Out of Manchester

■ ■ ■ Alton Towers
Alton, Stoke-on-Trent. 01538 703 344

This isn't just one for the kids – in fact, go without children otherwise you'll be stuck on the Squirrel Nutkin ride all day. My advice is follow the park round clockwise, starting with the 3D cinema to get your stomach ready then take the cable car across the Gloomy Wood to the X-Factor area. Take in all the big rides like Oblivion (the world's first vertical drop rollercoaster), Nemesis (60 seconds of extreme adrenaline) and Hex, which tells the story of the Towers ending in an optical illusion that will completely mess with your head.

Open 9am – dusk 31st March- 28th September 2002
Mon-Fri £17 Adults, £14 Children 4-12, Sat & Sun £22 Adults, £18 Children 4-12, under 4's go free.

■ ■ ■ Altrincham Ice Rink
Devonshire Road, Altrincham (0161) 926 8316

Great fun but really very dangerous. There's always some pesky 14yr olds that fly past at

100 mph, and you're bound to be put to shame by the toddlers. Go a couple of times secretly before you take a date here and you're bound to impress.

Sessions are 11-4, 7.30-10.30 Mon-Fri, 10-12, 2-4.30, 7.30-10.30 Sat, Sun
Entry £4.60 afternoon, £4.90 evenings and weekends.

▇ ▇ ■ Chester Zoo
Two miles north of Chester on A41
01244 380 280

The largest zoo in the UK and it certainly shows. Suffering from a significant drop in profits and semi-closed all due to foot and mouth for a large part of 2001, lets hope 2002 brings them better luck. Whether you are here for the monkeys or the elephants, you will almost certainly find yourself sidetracked by the bison or tigers and leave wondering where the monkeys are. A very long, very tiring but very worthwhile day out.
Open 10am-5pm.
Adults £9.50, Children aged 3-15 £7, Family ticket £34 for 5 people

▇ ▇ ■ Snowbombing
Call (0161) 610 2001 for details
www.snowbombing.com
Now when we use the term 'out of Manchester', it's a pretty broad remit we know. Even so, Switzerland might seem to be pushing it slightly. But there is logic behind this madness. Snowbombing basically takes the best bits – the best Manchester club nights (Electric Chair, Counter Culture, Sub Tub plus other big names from around the UK), the people and the atmosphere, and adds shovel loads of snow. Outgoing Travel bring you an essential event on any self-respecting clubber or snowboarder's calendar. 2001 saw 600 people burning the candle at both ends in Risoul in the French Alps – now Snowbombing 2002 is packing up and heading off to the stunning resort of Villars in Switzerland on April 6th 2002 for a week, where they've taken over the whole resort. Club nights and DJs to be confirmed. Check their website for futher details.

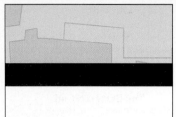

takeaway

www.itchymanchester.co.uk

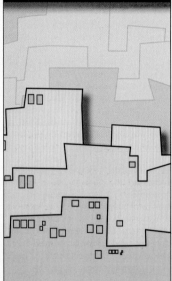

Pizza

Buy the Slice Pizza
2 Chapel Street (0161) 832 5553

Dominos
224 Wilmslow Road (0161) 257 3832

Pizza Express
95 Lapwing Lane, West Didsbury
(0161) 438 0838
6 South King Street (0161) 834 0145
56 Peter Street (0161) 839 9300
The Triangle (0161) 834 6130

Perfect Pizza
496 Wilbraham Road (0161) 881 4430

Pizzazz
786 Wilmslow Road (0161) 445 0010

Pizza Hut
Wilmslow Road (0161) 434 9920

Indian/Asian

Adbuls Kebabs
133 Oxford Road (0161) 273 7339
318 Wilmslow Road (0161) 248 7573

Gaylord Restaurant
Spring Gardens (0161) 832 6037

Great Kathmandu
Burton Road, West Didsbury
(0161) 434 6413

Sangam
Wilmslow Road, Rusholme
(0161) 224 8824

Raj's Indian Takeaway
290 Barlow Moor Road (0161) 861 8296

Oriental

Golden Rice Bowl
33a Cross Street (0161) 832 9033

Jade Garden
Wilmslow Road, Didsbury
(0161) 445 6979

New City Takeaway
220 Wilmslow Road (0161)224 2373

Gary, 20, Geologist

You look like a man who enjoys a Bacardi Breezer. True or false?
False – I drink bitter in Cord
In with the music crowd then?
Where's a cool place to go clubbing?
Correct. Usually to Roadhouse
Equally cool place to eat?
Ikan
Ha! Incorrect. And for shopping?
Afflecks rules
Hmm. Best thing about Manchester?
The facilities and ammenities
Interesting. And the worst?
Arrogance of the people.

Oriental Express
Stretford (0161) 865 8444
Centre (0161) 832 4646
South (0161) 945 4800

Fish and Chips

The Battered Cod
444 Wilmslow Road, Withington
(0161) 448 7520

The Chippy
50 Great Ancotes Street (0161) 228 0449

Churchill's Chippy
Canal Street (0161) 236 5529

The Crispy Cod
810 Wilmslow Road, Didsbury
(0161) 448 2468

Kingfisher Fish Bar
Tib Street (0161) 834 3332

Chicken

American Fried Chicken
43 Bloom Street (0161) 236 0276

Kansas Fried Chicken
701 Wilmslow Road (0161) 445 4557

McTucky Fried Chicken
40 Sackville Street (0161) 227 1337

Maxwin Fried Chicken
Oldham Street (0161) 950 2739

laters

www.itchymanchester.co.uk

Manchester is most definitely not a 24-hour city (still believing we should all be overcome by child-like excitement at the idea of a midnight feast). In fact, in compiling this, we've had to ask everyone we could think of… to come up with a pretty dismal array of places to be honest. Come on Manchester – get with it!

■ ■ ■ **Late night drinking** – At the weekend there are hundreds of places to drink late without door tax in Manchester – most café bars in this book in fact. Midweek, Deansgate Locks is always a good bet – any night there's somewhere open 'til 1am and no-one charges entry.

■ ■ ■ **Cigarettes at 4am?** – 24 hour Spar on Oxford Road and in Piccadilly. Tesco Metro on Market Street is 24-hours Mon-Fri. Another option in times of true full-on tobacco emergency are any of the hotels – try your hand at blagging (mates of ours have got everything from bog roll to a pint of milk on a good night). For that urgent need for Rizlas, pickled onion Monster Munch or Diet Coke there's also a smattering of 24-hour petrol stations (Wilmslow Road and Barlow Moor Road Chorlton).

■■■ **After-hours fridge stocking** – For the kind of munchies that only a trolley full of goodies can satisfy you've got the option of Tesco Metro in the town centre which is open 24-hours Mon-Fri, or Tesco in Parswood just outside Didsbury is also 24-hours (except on Sundays).

■■■ **Food now!** – There are hundreds of takeaways all over town which are open late, so this shouldn't be a problem. Abduls stay open forever, so they're always a safe bet.

■■■ **Nice food now!** – PerSia in The Great Northern serves food 'til about 12am – and it's excellent. The other option is the rather predictable one of Rusholme's curry mile – guaranteed eateries until at least 4am.

■■■ **Post club action** – Around kicking out time there's always primal cries of "shit I'm still buzzing – I need another drink". Creeks and paddles spring to mind because quite frankly Manchester doesn't cater well for those still active after 3am. There's the infamous Press Club, which is a total dive open all hours and full of the flotsam and jetsam of life – you can't be fussy though eh? Well, they apparently can – and you really have to be a face about town or a member to get in (or be exceptionally good at blagging). Another option is the Chinese Karaoke Bar (at the back of Princess Street). Again, not very salubrious but building up a cult-like status. Much more upmarket, but only on a Saturday night, is The Breakfast Club at Manto's which is open 'til 5am. Then there's Kais Chinese Restaurant – order the food, leave it (for your own sake) and buy four bottles of wine, then you're safe drinking until 4am. In fact most of China Town is open really late. As a last resort, club together for a hotel room – a tenner each between four and you've got a mini-members club and access to the hotel bar – sorted.

■■■ **Café Society** – We're woefully short of 24-hr cafés (namely harsh fluorescent lighting blinking mercilessly at your club-weathered skin). John Dalton Café is open into the early hours every night except Sunday . Take-out style cafes that stay open ridiculously late include Camel in Rusholme and Sam Sams in Hulme.

■■■ **Late night shopping** – Shops in the city centre are open until 6pm every night, except for Thursdays – where most places stay open until 9pm. The Triangle is open until 7pm every night. But for out of hours shopping, the mecca has to be The Trafford Centre as it's open until 9pm Mon-Fri, 7pm Sat, and 6pm Sun.

■■■ **Condoms/Tampons/Settlers** – There's a chemist on Oxford Road near the town hall - Cameolord, open 'til 12am every night. Lloyds in Fallowfield is open 'til 10.30pm.

accommodation

www.itchymanchester.co.uk

Prices are for one night, single room with breakfast.

For further info. call the Tourist Information 24 hour service. (0161) 264 3157/8

Quality

Crown Plaza
Peter Street (0161) 236 3333
Week £155, w/e £155

Malmasion
Gore Street (0161) 278 1000
Week £118.75, w/e £75+

Le Meridien Victoria & Albert
Water Street (0161) 832 1188
Week £165, w/e £94.50

The Portland Thistle Hotel
3-5 Portland Street (0161) 228 3400
Week £119, w/e £85

Renaissance Manchester Hotel
Blackfriars Street (0161) 835 3663
Week £99, w/e £75 (double)

Mid-price

Britannia Hotel
35 Portland Street (0161) 228 2288
Week £75, w/e £39.50

The Ox
Liverpool Road (0161) 839 7740
Week & w/e £44.95 (double)

▮ ▮ Cresent Gate Hotel
Park Cresent, Victoria Park, Rusholme
(0161) 224 0672
Week £38, w/e £38

▮ ▮ Mitre Hotel
Cathedral Gate (0161) 834 4128
Week £55, w/e £50

▮ ▮ Princess Hotel
101 Portland Street (0161) 236 5122
Week £57.50, w/e £57.50

▮ ▮ Budget

▮ ▮ The Burton Arms
31 Swan Street (0161) 834 3455
Week £30, w/e £30

▮ ▮ The Cornerhouse
Gravel Lane, Greengate (0161) 455 9988
Week £18, w/e £18

▮ ▮ Dolby Hotel
55 Blackfriers Road (0161) 907 2277
Week £38, w/e £38

▮ ▮ Merchants Hotel
Back Piccadilly (0161) 236 2939
Week £25, w/e £25

! 🗋 📎 From	Subject
✉ itchycity.co.uk	Weekend offers to your inbox

useful info

www.itchymanchester.co.uk

Travelling in and around Manchester
(In association with GMPTE)

The roads give you headaches, the parking gives you nightmares, and those pedestrians give you dents in your bonnet. You're best off leaving the motor at home if the truth be told. However, don't despair – Manchester offers a public transport network:

Rail: the city is served by two main rail stations, Manchester Piccadilly and Manchester Victoria, which are supported by other stations around the centre; Oxford Road, Deansgate and Salford Central.

Metrolink Tram: provides a link through the centre of Manchester with on-street stations around the Piccadilly Gardens area and at St Peter's Square. The trams also run out to Bury in the North, Altrincham in the South and Salford Quays and Eccles in the West (Eccles also boasts a huge park and ride site).

Bus: the main bus terminal is located within the Piccadilly Gardens area with buses leaving every few minutes to hundreds of destinations (for full information contact GMPTE – details below). A free shuttle bus runs around the city centre. Starting and finishing its trips at Piccadilly Rail Station, it links the Piccadilly area with King Street,

Deansgate and the new M&S store, the Triangle and The Printworks. See map for more details.

GMPTE, the local authority on public transport in Greater Manchester, provide a website containing all the info you will ever need on travelling around Manchester. Visit them at **www.gmpte.com**.

Technophobes and those frankly lonely people can talk to someone on...

GMPTE (8am-8pm) ....(0161) 228 7811
Train enquiries............................08457 484950
Metrolink ....(0161) 205 2000

■ ■ ■ Useful Telephone numbers

Shopmobility

Altrincham	(0161) 9291714
Rochdale	(01706) 865986
Ashton....................................	(01942) 724910
Stockport................................	(0161) 6661100
Bolton	(01204) 392946
Trafford Centre	(0161) 7491728
Bury	(0161) 7649966
Wigan.....................................	(01942) 825520
Leigh	(01942) 683163
Hyde	(0161) 3689600
Manchester	(0161) 8394060
Oldham	(0161) 6330040

■ ■ ■ Planes

Manchester Airport ....(0161) 489 3000

■ ■ ■ Taxis

Black cabs

Mantax	(0161) 236 5133
Taxifone	(0161) 236 2322
Radio Cars	(0161) 236 8033
Saltax	(0161) 737 2222

Private Hire

Call-A-Cab	(0161) 320 7117
Carriages	(0161) 220 7770

Getting a cab at 2am

Newton Street – Roadhouse (outside) you'll catch the empty cabs going up towards Piccadilly Gardens.

Oldham Street – well, you can dream. Anywhere along **Oxford Road** has many empty cabs returning from Didsbury and Withington. You're sure to get one eventually, and if not, there's loads of buses travelling up and down.

Piccadilly Gardens is full of lime shirts and short skirts and the queue can be a dangerous place to be, but it is one of the only places you are absolutely guaranteed to get a cab if you're prepared to wait for hours.

Areas such as **Minshull Street** and **Ducie Street** should be avoided as it's a red-light and generally dodgy area. It's certainly not recommended for women alone.

itchy tells you where, the bus gets you there

There's **better** things to spend **money** on.
Don't waste it on travel.

If you're under 26 or a student save £££'s on travel with a Young Persons' Discount Coachcard. Cards cost £9 and save you up to 30% off already low fares all year. Register online to receive special offers throughout the year.

For journey planning, tickets and coachcards

visit **GoByCoach.com** or call 08705 80 80 80

NATIONAL EXPRESS »

Check online for details.
Coach services depart from Lever Street Bus Station (up to 24th March 2002),
then Chorlton Street Coach Station, Manchester .

Citicars-Scorpio	(0161) 795 8080
Concorde	(0161) 371 7777
Didsbury	(0161) 445 7700
Kingsway	(0161) 445 2454
New City Cars	(0161) 236 5000
New Link	(0161) 445 3399
New United	(0161) 225 8502
Supacars	(0161) 445 5000
Village Cars	(0161) 237 3383

■ ■ Coaches
National Express 08705 808080
See advert for address
Stagecoach ....(0161) 228 7811

■ ■ Tourist Information
Manchester ....(0161) 234 3157

■ ■ Car hire
Budget 0800 181 181
Hertz ....(0161) 236 2747
Salford Car Hire ....(0161) 833 9311

■ ■ Manchester Media

■ ■ Entertainments & Listings
itchy Manchester – Obviously you've bought the book (if you've stolen it, borrowed it or are currently reading it in the shop – shame on you), but if you want to be right up to date with events, articles and previews, you really should be visiting *itchymanchester.co.uk* regularly.

City Life – Published fortnightly and containing full listings, reviews and articles (great for all things musical) – this magazine's an essential read for any self-respecting man/woman about town.

Go – free supplement to MEN on a Friday evening, all about entertainment, with reviews, previews and listings. Bit thin on the ground for info, but worth reading.

Cash Points

Portland Street, Natwest: Opp. top of Chorlton St
Arndale, Natwest: Fountain St just off Market St
Oxford Road: HSBC: Opp. Spar/ Revolution
NQ, Link: Corner Market Street/ Oldham St
Piccadilly, Natwest: Piccadilly Gardens, Lloyds and HSBC in the station
Castlefield, Link: By the bar in Barca
The Gay Village, Barclays: Whitworth Street / Princess St corner

itchy tells you where, the tram gets you there

■ ■ ■ Local Newspapers

Manchester Evening News – Speaks for itself – news, in the evening, about Manchester. Pretty difficult crossword.

Metro – Oh this'll confuse you. There's one free daily Metro given out on buses, train stations etc. It's a tabloid much like the Metro in Leeds and London, and generally speaking, it's a cracking read with a combination of national and local news. Then there's Friday's Metro, which is delivered to homes across Manchester. This is more your kind of cat stuck up tree type news. Good for buying, selling and snoozing.

■ ■ ■ Student Media

Grip – UMIST's own magazine. Unusually large paper, wonderfully glossy, surprisingly low on actual content but stylistically excellent. Infrequent publication with dubious readership.

Student Direct – The big daddy. Based at Manchester University but circulated to Salford, UMIST and Bolton too. Weekly inky with the usual student news, features,

reviews etc. Long established and still shines. High standard of writing makes up for the occasionally tedious design.

Pulp – Manchester Met's magazine, produced after controversial opt-out from the Student Direct fold. Generally lacklustre but with great potential. The new editor has a big job on his hands. Too shiny to wipe your arse on though.

Fuse FM – Manchester University's newly established radio station. Initial broadcasts revealed scores of Mark and Lard wannabes but some genuinely great alternative radio.

■ ■ ■ Radio

Galaxy 102 – Manchester's number one choice for dance and R'n'B, aimed at young Manchester and those who don't take life too seriously.

Key 103 – Another local commercial station for Manchester with it's unique local style and a number of good DJs. Is involved with club nights around the city.

■ ■ ■ TV

BBC North – dominating Oxford Road, hang around outside for glimpses of Mark and Lard or the likes of Vanessa Feltz…

Granada – based in Manchester and producers of some fine TV – shame the Granada Tours are now closed.

Manchester TV – don't be fooled by promises that MTV will be in attendance at various events around Manchester – it's not the glamorous one – it's the shitty local station that most people don't even know about, let alone watch.

itchy tells you where, the train gets you there

Travelling in and around Manchester by Public Transport

How to get more information:

Internet: www.gmpte.com - all the info you will ever need and a journey planner to boot!

Telephone: 0161–228 7811 (8am to 8pm daily) – our transport experts are waiting to help you.

0161–242 6040 (24 hr answerphone) – order leaflets & timetables to be sent to you.

GMPTE Travelshops: located in Piccadilly Gardens and at major bus stations around the county, these useful outlets sell most multi-journey tickets, can help you with your public transport queries and stock most of GMPTE's timetables, maps and other leaflets.

itchy tells you where, GMPTE gets you there

GMPTE

index

✳ **KEY103 feel the noise**

☀ KEY103 feel the noise

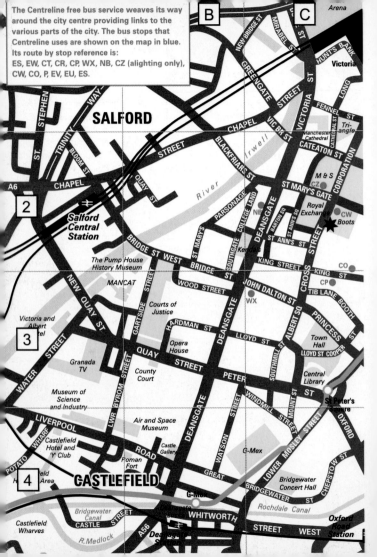

The Centreline free bus service weaves its way around the city centre providing links to the various parts of the city. The bus stops that Centreline uses are shown on the map in blue. Its route by stop reference is:
ES, EW, CT, CR, CP, WX, NB, CZ (alighting only), CW, CO, P, EV, EU, ES.

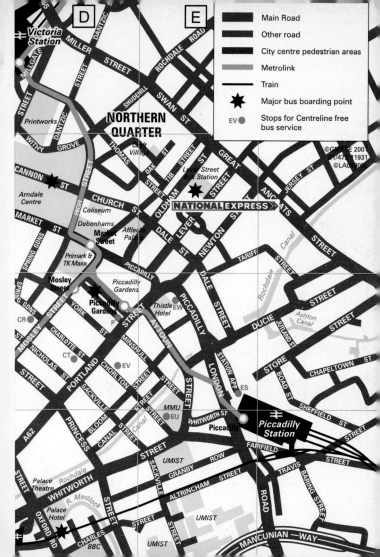